MW01122954

PENGUIN BOOKS

MAINE PARADISE

Writer/photographer Russell D. Butcher has been a conservation specialist for the National Audubon Society, a writer for the Save-the-Redwoods League, a research editor for the Sierra Club, and author of numerous articles and books, including *New Mexico: Gift of the Earth* and *The Desert*. Mr. Butcher was for many years a resident of Seal Harbor, Maine.

Marie Ivey Menzietti, also a long-time resident of Seal Harbor, is a freelance artist and photographer.

MAINE PARADISE

Mount Desert Island and Acadia National Park

by

Russell D. Butcher

Drawings by

Marie Ivey Menzietti

Photographs by
the Author and the Artist

Prelude by
Carl W. Buchheister
President Emeritus
National Audubon Society

PENGUIN BOOKS

Acknowledgments

I am deeply grateful to my wife, Pam, whose constant faith, enthusiasm, and editorial assistance never wavered, and who is the other half of the "we" in much of the text. A very special thanks also to our Mount Desert friends—Kay and Franz Karban, and Pat and Neal Bousfield; to Carl W. Buchheister for his Prelude; to Maurice Sullivan and Paul G. Favour, Jr., former chief naturalists at Acadia National Park; and to my parents, Mary and Devereux Butcher, who introduced me to this island many years ago. And a special word of appreciation to Sigurd F. Olson of Ely, Minnesota, and to Nicolas Ducrot and Mary Velthoven of The Viking Press.   R.D.B.

With gratitude to my husband, Tony, for his love and encouragement. And special thanks to Jean Feigley, Donna Louise Feigley, Elise Witham, George Chambers, Jane Rupp, and Nicolas Ducrot.

Seal Harbor, Maine, October 1972   M.I.M.

Penguin Books Ltd, Harmondsworth, Middlesex, England
Penguin Books, 40 West 23rd Street, New York, New York 10010, U.S.A.
Penguin Books Australia Ltd, Ringwood, Victoria, Australia
Penguin Books Canada Limited, 2801 John Street, Markham, Ontario, Canada L3R 1B4
Penguin Books (N.Z.) Ltd, 182–190 Wairau Road, Auckland 10, New Zealand

First published in the United States of America by The Viking Press 1973
Viking Compass Edition published 1975
Reprinted 1975
Published in Penguin Books 1976
Reprinted 1978, 1987

LIBRARY OF CONGRESS CATALOGING IN PUBLICATION DATA
Butcher, Russell D.
Maine paradise.
Bibliography: p. 95.
1. Mount Desert Island. 2. Acadia National Park.
I. Menzietti, Marie Ivey. II. Title.
[F27.M9B87 1976]   917.41′45   76-20770
ISBN 0 14 00.4316 0

Printed in the United States of America by
Halliday Lithograph Corporation, West Hanover, Massachusetts
Illustrations printed by Rae Publishing Co., Inc., Cedar Grove, New Jersey
Set in Linotype De Vinne

Acknowledgment is made to the following for permission to quote from
the sources indicated.

J. B. Lippincott Co. and Collins-Knowlton-Wing, Inc.: From *Homeland:
A Report from the Country* by Hal Borland. Copyright © 1969
by Hal Borland. Reprinted by permission.

Oxford University Press: From *A Sand County Almanac* by Aldo Leopold.

Contents

For Pam and Tony
with Love

Prelude

Of the thirteen states along the U.S. Atlantic seaboard, Maine possesses a coast so different from the others that it is as if it belonged to another country. Sand beaches extend from Key West, Florida, all the way north to Massachusetts. Then, almost abruptly, the famed rockbound coast of Maine begins.

It is not only the rocky shore that makes Maine's coast unusual. It is also the irregularity of its contours—extending 225 miles from Kittery to Eastport, yet winding more than 2500 miles into many scores of bays and coves and out around as many peninsulas and points of land. And the coast of Maine is unusual for its innumerable rocky islands—from the smallest ledges and tiny spruce-covered isles to massive Mount Desert.

Surrounding these coastal islands, the waters of the sea are cold, kept that way by the Labrador Current that sweeps into the Gulf of Maine, and by the great tides that cause a constant upwelling from the dark depths below. While the water may be too frigid for enjoyable summer swimming, its temperature is of enormous importance to all the myriad forms of marine life. For the colder it is, the greater is its oxygen content and the greater the abundance of life that the water can sustain. Among this abundance are incredible quantities of minute plants and animals, drifting in the upper surface waters and carried along with the tides and currents.

Collectively, these tiny microscopic organisms, called plankton, form the vast "pastures of the sea," the most plentiful and basic food resource of the marine environment. It is upon them that all the other creatures of the sea, from the smallest fish to the mighty blue whale, directly or indirectly depend for their survival. And in turn, this abundant life in the sea provides food for a great variety of birdlife—the gulls and terns, scoters and eiders, and auks and petrels. The spectacle of these seabirds congregating in great colonies each summer to rear their young on the outer coastal islands of Maine adds another dimension to the beauty and wonder of Mount Desert Island itself, which the author of this book so eloquently describes.

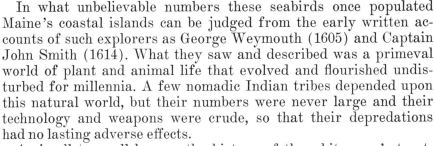

In what unbelievable numbers these seabirds once populated Maine's coastal islands can be judged from the early written accounts of such explorers as George Weymouth (1605) and Captain John Smith (1614). What they saw and described was a primeval world of plant and animal life that evolved and flourished undisturbed for millennia. A few nomadic Indian tribes depended upon this natural world, but their numbers were never large and their technology and weapons were crude, so that their depredations had no lasting adverse effects.

As is all too well known, the history of the white man's treatment of the land has its often-repeated ugly chapters. Sadly, the coast of Maine was no exception. It is well to recall a little of this story here, because the thoughtlessness and greed of the past were instrumental in bringing us to a different age, led by such groups as the Audubon societies.

Not long after the European immigrants settled along America's East Coast, the rape of Maine's island seabird colonies began. The eggs of gulls and other species were gathered for food—at first, here and there, but then with increasing fervor and thoroughness. Egging was carried on as if the supply were inexhaustible; no one gave thought to the welfare of the species. Consequently, under the impact of egging and related disturbances, the bird populations began to decline.

Then a still more devastating practice descended upon the island bird colonies. Fashion, the most powerful of dictators, demanded more and more plumage for the millinery trade, and the gulls and terns of Maine were among its principal victims. Both the native Indians and white man invaded the island nurseries during the summer months, killing the parent birds and leaving their eggs and young to perish. A crueler and more lethal method of exploitation could hardly have been devised.

As great barrels filled with the bodies of dead birds were brought to the villages of the inhabited islands and mainland, scores of women were employed to prepare the skins, keeping their feathers intact. After being treated with alum, salt, and preservatives, the skins were packed in cases and shipped aboard coastal sailing vessels to New York City, the major center of the booming, multimillion-dollar millinery industry.

For many years thousands upon thousands of these birds were slaughtered. After visiting Mount Desert Island in the summer

of 1900, William Dutcher, who was chairman of the American Ornithologists' Union's Committee on Bird Protection, wrote to a member of the Maine state legislature: "An Indian gunner at Bar Harbor informed me that no less than 10,000 gulls were shot in Maine by Indians during the season of 1899 for shipment to Boston and New York City, for use as millinery ornaments."

In fact, by the turn of the century, following three hundred years of egging and slaughter, the summer islands of Maine that had once been so crowded with avian life had virtually become biological deserts.

Fortunately, a new age was now dawning in the thought and conscience of man, as reflected in some new activities along the coast of Maine. At the same time that individuals on Mount Desert were beginning to explore how they might preserve the natural beauty of that island for posterity, the first few steps were being taken toward protecting the coastal birds. In 1900 Dutcher engaged a Captain Driscoll, head keeper of Great Duck Island light station, about six miles out beyond Mount Desert, to protect the birds on nearby Little Duck Island, which had long been a favorite of the plume hunters.

In the same year the arctic tern colony on far-out Matinicus Rock, some thirty-five miles southwest of Mount Desert, was given similar protection by its head lightkeeper, while the owner of a tiny island in the Matinicus Archipelago, called No Man's Land, was hired to protect gulls nesting there. These early Maine wildlife wardens did much to advance a new, but at that time extremely unpopular, gospel of conservation—a gospel that germinated in the fertile soil of the humane reaction to the slaughter, the cruelty, and the greed. With it began the Audubon movement, starting with the Massachusetts Audubon Society in 1896. Within three years there were sixteen similar groups: in New Hampshire, Rhode Island, Connecticut, New York, New Jersey, and even in far-off Texas and California. The appalling destruction of the island-nesting birds of Maine did more to trigger this movement than did any other killing of birdlife elsewhere in the country.

Next, the indefatigable Dutcher and his committee, aided by the Audubon societies, began successfully to encourage the passage of bird protection laws through the legislatures of many states and to fight against and ultimately defeat the feather trade

—a landmark conservation victory that was accomplished with the indispensable and powerful influence of women everywhere. By 1905 the National Association of Audubon Societies (later becoming the National Audubon Society) was incorporated, with Dutcher as its president, and soon the new organization had fourteen wardens stationed along the coast of Maine alone.

The islands were finally safe once again. With man's destructive pressures gone, the birds began to return to their ancestral haunts and increase their numbers. Today most of these species have largely regained their former abundance.

Now, on a day in June, as one approaches Matinicus Rock, where the farthest lighthouse off the coast signals the approaches to Penobscot Bay, one sees against the sky a blizzard of snowy white wings of the arctic terns, hovering and fluttering over their nesting ground. From the reports of lightkeepers and a few visiting ornithologists over the years, we have had positive evidence of the existence of this colony for the past century. One of the highlights of the year for the lightkeepers and their families at the Rock was the custom of staying up late into the nights, beginning about the tenth of May, to await the return of the ''Medricks,'' as the coastal people call the terns.

For those who lived on that lonely Rock knew it was always at about that time in May that these birds would come out of the night in a great wheeling, swarming, crying mass. After just a few hours on the island, they would fly out to sea again. Each day following they would return, staying a little longer each time. By the end of a week the terns would finally settle down to mating and raising their young.

The selection of mates is preceded by an elaborate courtship, one of the most stirring acts of which is the lovely, graceful flight of a male and female together. High up in the sky they sail on motionless wings, which in their closeness seem at times to touch —a *pas de deux* of an awesomely beautiful aerial ballet.

Small wonder, then, that the men and women of the light station rejoiced over the return of these ''swallows of the sea,'' that heralded the end of the long, lonely, and lifeless winter months.

When the breeding season is over, near the end of summer, the arctic terns begin their unbelievable migration to their wintering grounds. Leaving the coast of Maine, they fly eastward around

Nova Scotia, northward past Newfoundland, then across the Atlantic, finally heading south, passing Ireland, the coasts of Europe and Africa, to reach their destination at and beyond the Antarctic Circle. There these birds spend the winter months in the Antarctic summer. Their annual round-trip migration covers roughly 25,000 miles, making them the world's champion long-distance fliers.

Before we leave Matinicus Rock, we must mention a bird which is unique to it, to Maine, and to the entire United States—the Atlantic puffin. This member of the auk family, with its black back and white underparts, is distinguished by its triangular, parrotlike beak that is brightly colored with red, yellow, and blue. As far as we know, Matinicus Rock is the only place in the United States where this droll-looking little bird nests, and there are approximately 250 of them there. Every summer people come in increasing numbers, hiring fishermen at considerable expense to take them out to see this one bird. Because of the difficulties involved, the human visitors seldom land on the Rock. They cruise around and around, observing the puffins sitting in groups on the water, buzzing back and forth like oversize bumblebees on their short wings, or standing erect on the island. Their nests are hidden in dark recesses of the rocks, and they feed only on fish which they pursue by "flying" under water, propelling themselves with their wings and steering with their red webbed feet. The puffin is rare along the Maine coast, but is abundant farther north—on islands off the Canadian Maritimes, Iceland, Scandinavia, and the British Isles.

Off Mount Desert, on Little Duck and a few other islands, there is a summering bird so seldom seen that its existence is known only to a few. That is because it is nocturnal in going to and from its island home. It is the Leach's petrel, a bird with all the mystery and romantic aura of the sea. Known to English-speaking men of the sea as Mother Carey's chicken, it is a truly pelagic bird, never coming to land except to raise its young. The ocean is its real element; there it drinks the saltwater, derives all its food from the surface, and sleeps.

This petrel is only eight inches long and is a dark sooty color all over except for a white patch on its rump. Way out at sea one sees the petrels in flight—a bounding flight that they can maintain for incredible lengths of time. One can't help but wonder how they survive great storms that sweep across the ocean.

11

When the petrel hovers low over the water to feed, its little black webbed feet hang down, and it looks for all the world as if it were walking on the water. It is said that the petrel was named after Saint Peter, who walked on the water, and doubtless this association must have some foundation, for an old-timer on the coast responded once to my description of the bird by calling it a "walking-Peter."

Only a very few of the Leach's petrels nest as far south as Massachusetts; furthermore, it can nest only on islands on which there are no predatory mammals. Since it builds its nests in little subterranean burrows or tunnels which it digs in the earth, it would soon be eliminated by foxes, skunks, weasels, and rats. The larger gulls—the herring and great black-backed—are its principal enemies on the islands, and the petrel's nocturnal habits are designed at least partly to enable it to escape the gulls that would kill them if they flew to and from their breeding places in broad daylight.

If one should spend the night, especially a dark foggy one, on a petrel island off Mount Desert, one would be struck with wonder at the ability of these birds, coming from several hundred miles at sea, to find not only their island but their own particular hole in the ground.

This amazing and mysterious power of orientation has been tested and studied for many years at the Bowdoin College Scientific Station on Kent Island, located just off Canada's Grand Manan Island at the eastern end of the Maine coast. This narrow island is covered only with grass and low-growing spruces, but beneath the jumble of trees the ground is filled with the burrows of petrels. In one particular scientific experiment eleven of the little birds were carefully taken from their nests and small numbered bands were placed around their legs, with their burrows correspondingly numbered. The petrels were then placed in a box, rushed to Halifax, Nova Scotia, and put aboard a jet bound for Prestwick, Scotland. Upon arrival, they were immediately taken down to the sea and released, only twenty-four hours after being taken from Kent Island.

Nine days later one of them returned to its nest! Averaging about 300 miles of flight per day, it had followed a course it had never flown before, over a vast unmarked expanse of ocean, and somehow zeroed in on its tiny hole in the ground among literally dozens of similar holes in the dense spruce forest. Seven of the original petrels ultimately succeeded in making that 3000-mile journey.

Contemplating the remarkable feat of the petrel, and all the other mysteries of nature, one is filled with a sense of wonder and is humbled by the realization that behind everything in nature there is Order, an inexorable law. Therein lies the greatest beauty of all.

I have often visited Mount Desert Island over the years. In few other places is nature more prodigal in her gifts, or man more in harmony with his surroundings. The great bird colonies of the nearby outer islands have been restored, and a magnificent natural heritage in Acadia National Park has been saved through the generosity of many people on Mount Desert, for the enjoyment of all people.

May this book, created with such love, beauty, and understanding, become a *vade mecum* for all fortunate enough to visit or live on Mount Desert Island.

Bethesda, Maryland
October 1972

Carl W. Buchheister
President Emeritus
National Audubon Society

MAINE PARADISE

The Sun's First Rays

A narrow band of light along the eastern horizon slowly spread and brightened. Faintly at first, we began to make out the ragged edge of a darkly forested land and clusters of islands, contrasting with long bays, sheltered coves, and the open ocean. Gradually we became aware of textures and colors —the wind-ruffled silver water, a hint of green in the forests, and smooth rock surfaces of the mountains.

While the scene, spread out below us, was still in the shadow of the earth's turning, our mountaintop vantage point was suddenly and silently touched, then flooded with the sun's first golden light. As its warmth inched slowly downward, low clumps of windswept spruce trees cast long, dark shadows that seemed etched into the expanses of rock.

One by one, the barren summits of the lower mountains, stretching ridge upon ridge to the east and west across the island, were crowned with the sunlight that advanced steadily lower. Great rounded shadows of the mountains reached across the intervening valleys, and slowly they diminished, until finally the lakes and ponds, which earlier had been as calm as glass, now sparkled in the sunshine. The ocean beyond turned brilliant blue, and the dawn was complete.

The 1530-foot summit of Cadillac Mountain, the highest point along the United States Atlantic coast, is the first place in the country to be hit by the sun's rays. From here we could see much that makes Mount Desert, Maine's largest coastal island, one of the most beautiful and varied landscapes to be found anywhere—uniquely combining mountains, lakes, forests, and seashore, all within its 108 square miles. As we looked out across the island, we thought of the many miles of trails and carriage roads that wind throughout the wild forests, past lakes and bogs, along great ocean cliffs, or that scale sheer cliffs to the mountain summits. We thought of the changing seasons—the sudden rush of springtime, the all-too-short summer, the glory of autumn, and the wildness of winter.

We thought of the courage, ingenuity, and dedication of the generous individuals who helped save 46 square miles of the island's outstanding natural landscapes within Acadia—a national park that today ranks behind only Great Smoky Mountains and Grand Teton in annual visitation. And we thought of the long history of Mount Desert—its Indian summer encampments, discovery by explorers from Europe, international territorial disputes, settlement by a rugged, self-reliant people, and the early summer "rusticators."

We thought, too, of the present island people—the 8000 year-round residents, the 15,000 to 20,000 summer residents, and the great multitudes of visitors, all of whom, in spite of steadily rising numbers over the years, still make a relatively small impact upon the face of the island. The hand of man on Mount Desert and the coast of Maine, unlike most other popular places in the world, has so far caused little harm. In fact, much of what has been done over the decades to build year-round communities, businesses, summer homes, and research and educational institutions, for the most part fits harmoniously into the total scene. Architectural styles and building materials used in construction have, with few exceptions, provided added interest and a simple, rustic charm that reflects the natural setting.

Perhaps this is part of the story of Acadia National Park, of Mount Desert Island, and the coast of Maine—that man has proved he need not ruin an environment in order to live there, that the natural and man-made elements can exist side by side, each complementing the other. The key is that people must care, and care enough . . . and that is really what this island is all about.

The Sculptured Land

During the most recent Ice Age, some 20,000 years ago, a great continental glacier, several thousand feet thick, advanced slowly southward from the Arctic all across northeastern North America, covering Minnesota, the Great Lakes region, New York, and New England.

At Mount Desert the glacier moved southeastward toward the sea . . . until its progress was blocked at right angles by a mountain range trending from northeast to southwest. The tremendous tide of ice at first backed up behind this barrier. Then it surged gradually up and over the crest of the range. As the flood became larger and the weight and pressures more intense, the ice poured through low places and flowed in long fingers down stream valleys on the seaward side. Finally, the mountains and all the surrounding countryside were completely buried beneath several thousand feet of the glacier.

The granite rock of the range, which several hundred million years earlier had been created from the slow cooling of a fiercely hot intrusion of molten magma within the earth, was now gradually being rounded off and smoothed into the present gentle contours. As the ice ground its way through the lower mountain passes, it wore them down into U-shaped valleys, separated from each other by the remaining north-side ridges of the former range.

Great sheer cliffs were formed along the southeastern side of many of the mountains, for the ice, pouring over the summits, quarried great blocks of granite as it flowed off the other sides, thus creating the escarpments of Beech, St. Sauveur, Jordan, the South Bubble, the Beehive, and Champlain mountains.

After the glacial age ended and the ice slowly melted, water collected in the troughs of the valleys, creating many of the island's lakes and ponds. One valley was cut more deeply along its entire length, and when the sea came to its present level, with the melting of the continental glacier and rebounding of the land, it flooded this valley, forming the only fjord on the U.S. Atlantic coast.

There is evidence, too, that the great weight of the ice actually depressed the island and the entire coast by a hundred feet or more. Several levels of ancient sea cliffs and beaches have been discovered to at least 500 feet above the present sea level, indicating long intervals in which the ocean level stayed at particular elevations higher on the mountainsides.

The melting glacier also left behind tremendous quantities of gravel and great boulders, called glacial erratics. Many of these erratics lie about on the mountain summits, and one of the most prominent appears precariously perched on the South Bubble, still exactly where the glacier left it thousands of years ago.

Through aeons of geologic time the shape of the land has been changing constantly. Great periods of mountain building by forces deep within the earth have been followed by long intervals of gradual erosion. Through it all, the sea has invaded and withdrawn, its level rising and falling and rising again with the great rhythms of the universe. So it is that the present coast of Maine is now higher and farther inland than it has been. Once there were stream valleys that are now the hundreds of sheltered bays, harbors, and coves. There were ridges that are now long peninsulas jutting into the sea, while farther out there were hilltops that remain as the scatterings of islands in the sea, with Mount Desert the largest of them all.

Along the edge of the shore are sloping ledges of pink crystalline granite made up of quartz, feldspar, and other minerals; while darker rock, called breccia and diorite, form sheer cliffs and headlands. Here and there are coves with beaches and seawalls of smoothly rounded cobblestones, where the rocks grind against each other as the waves crash in and ebb away.

There are only two sand beaches on the island. One is at Seal Harbor where a scene of moored sailing and fishing boats is framed by spruce-covered points and low-lying outer islands. The other is Sand Beach which forms a barrier across the cove at Great Head. Here fine grains of sand are mixed with unusually large amounts of tiny particles of shell which are constantly washed up by ocean currents. On a sunny day the shallower water becomes a brilliant green against the sand beneath, contrasting with the blue of the deeper sea beyond. Behind the beach is a rolling crest of dunes and waving dune grass, while a freshwater pool ringed by cattails and bulrushes is trapped behind. When this beach is free of sunbathers, flocks of tiny sanderlings dart in unison in search of food with each withdrawing wave.

There are trails along the shore from here, inviting exploration. From atop Great Head, a panorama unrolls of the open ocean and far up Frenchman Bay. Beyond Egg Rock Light lies mainland Schoodic Peninsula; while close to shore swirling flocks of gulls trail behind an occasional bobbing lobster boat.

Framing a shore path that follows Ocean Drive two miles to Otter Point is a grove of twisted pitch pines that stands picturesquely above the fractured granite ledges. When the sea and tide are right at Thunder Hole, the surf rushes into a deep cleft in the rocks, making a muffled booming that is as much felt as heard.

Continuing on, the trail soon enters a dark spruce forest that is rich with soft green moss and tufts of hanging beard lichen where parula warblers make their nests in summer. Windstorms have toppled many of the tall trees here, and where the sunlight reaches the ground in these openings, thick clumps of young spruces and firs are crowding in to take their place. Then, climbing a little, the path emerges onto the top of Otter Cliffs, the highest ocean cliffs on the U.S. Atlantic coast, affording a sweeping view back along the rugged shore.

In a winter storm this edge of the sea is transformed into a place of awesome violence and fury. The gray-green water rolls in on a rising tide, bursting again and again upon the rocks in great white geysers of spray that leap high into the air. With the temperature far below freezing, the ledges become coated with ice, and great masses of icicles hang from the cliffs. Just offshore, a thousand eider ducks ride the huge swells.

Twice daily, along the rocky shore, the ten-foot drop from flood tide to ebb reveals a hidden community of plants and animals. At the upper edge of the intertidal zone grow vast colonies of white barnacles—a form of crustacean that is strangely related to the crab and lobster. Within thick forests of waving brown seaweeds—the beaded rockweed and bladder wrack—live colonies of periwinkles, dog whelks, and limpets. In tide pools bright with green and yellow encrusting sponges and pale rose algae are starfish, brittle stars, mussels, sea urchins, sea anemones, and Jonah crabs. Farther down, where fewer of the sun's rays reach, there are the red seaweeds—dulse and Irish moss—while just below the low-tide line is another zone of brown seaweeds—the kelps and others with long leathery fronds.

All the living things of this demanding environment have evolved not only to withstand the tremendous pounding and pulling of the sea, but to survive the alternate exposure to water and air. It is a place, says Rachel Carson, "of compromise and conflict and eternal change," "a world that keeps alive the sense of continuing creation and of the relentless drive of life."

On the western side of Mount Desert there are other inviting walks along the shore . . . such as the nature trail at Ship Harbor. This sheltered cove is completely emptied of the sea at low tide; the water rushes in and out of its mouth like the flowing of a river. Along the outer granite shore nearby there are wild roses, beach peas, and seaside goldenrod, while the tangy salt air is mixed with the fragrances of spruce and pine, the spicy bayberry, and the distinctive faint aroma of crowberry, a tiny ground-covering plant of the Arctic that by some mystery extends its range to the cooler parts of coastal Maine.

Other edges of the sea are the shallow coves of Frenchman and Blue Hill bays, the clam flats where at low tide the long-legged great blue herons hunt for food in summer. And there are the salt marsh meadows along the tidal creeks and inlets . . . above Bass Harbor, Somes Sound, and at Pretty Marsh where cord grass, spike grass, salt hay grass, and glasswort grow. These coastal wetlands are the rich breeding places for many kinds of finfish and shellfish and smaller aquatic organisms that are indispensable to the intricate web of marine life. And then there are those links between the sea and the freshwater lakes of the land—the alewives, anadramous fish of the herring family, which mysteriously migrate up a few of the island's streams each spring to spawn in such places as Seal Cove Pond.

The Rush of Spring

Spring comes reluctantly to Mount Desert Island. With a hesitant but welcome hint in early March, chickadees and song sparrows begin to sing their first few musical notes. Snow still lies deep upon the mountains, and the lakes and ponds are frozen solid. Yet, even as winter sends its last flurries of snow and sleet down upon the land, there is the barely perceptible change, of maple buds starting to swell and birch catkins expanding.

It is the first gurgling song of the red-winged blackbird from a cattail marsh, though, that really seems to signal the long-awaited arrival of slightly warming days. Now the snow melts more quickly from the mountains, leaving only pockets of white up along the ledges where a month ago it blanketed the bald summits. April rains add to the melting, and brooks become dashing torrents that fill the forests with the sound of waterfalls.

By mid-April we hear flocks of Canada geese passing overhead, honking as they fly to shallows of nearby bays on their long trek northward to summer breeding grounds. And then the great blue herons are back, wading in the tidal inlets, where a piercing cry draws our attention upward to an osprey circling. Before the month is out, the great sheets of ice disappear from lakes and ponds, and the loons return from coastal waters, their wild calls echoing between the mountainsides.

In early May, as the first flush of maple flowers finally spreads across the forest, we hear the clear high notes of the white-throated sparrow, singing, "Old Sam Peabody, Peabody, Peabody." Then suddenly the season's tempo quickens, unfolding with a rush. Birds from distant wintering places in South and Central America and the southern states pour in overnight to fill the woods with choruses of song. There are the thrushes and warblers, vireos and flycatchers, and finches, grosbeaks, and tanagers. From the dark spruce forests tumbles a wild cascade of song of the secretive winter wren. In the hush of dusk, after the liquid vespers of the wood and hermit thrushes have ended, there sometimes comes the endlessly repeated call of a bird seldom seen, the whippoorwill.

One of the surprises of mid-May, just as green leaves are beginning to unfurl, is the emergence of an unpretentious shrubby tree we have ignored all year. The shadbush, covered with masses of delicate white flowers, now stands out from the rest of the forest. Paddling our canoe up Great (Long) Pond, we have seen their curtains of white reflected in the still water, contrasting with dark forms of ancient hemlocks and tall white pines. On returning to this place a few days later, we could find no hint of where the shads had been.

By the end of May, as lilacs and apple trees come into bloom around the island, our search begins for the pinkish-white arbutus. One year we found our first in a sunny glade beside a pond. There the clusters of shy flowers were half-hidden amid their bed of dark green leaves, and we knelt down to catch a whiff of their unforgettable faint fragrance.

As the pace of wildflower succession increases, our walks through the forests reveal clumps of purple violets along stream banks where fern fiddleheads unroll. Thick patches of delicate pale bluets cover grassy openings, while once in a while we find clusters of pink lady's slippers blooming beneath a grove of pines.

It is a joyous time of discovery on Mount Desert, when the mystery and wonder of life's renewal are everywhere.

Meeting of North and South

The forests of Mount Desert have a special quality, one that is explained in part by the exceptional variety of trees and smaller plant life, representing widely differing life zones and climatic conditions. Here the northern coniferous and temperate deciduous forests meet and overlap, with additional varieties of flora of the treeless Arctic tundra far to the north and others that reach no farther north than here.

The scattered sphagnum-heath peat bogs of the island are little post-Ice Age remnants of the tundra world. They are carpeted with spongy green and red cushions of sphagnum moss, on which grow crowberry, sweet gale, baked-appleberry, and the delicate arethusa and grass-pink orchids. Here, too, are the strange carnivorous plants—the pitcher plant and round-leaf sundew which have evolved methods of capturing and absorbing insects. Throughout the bogs grow a few members of the heath family, including Labrador tea, whose white-flowered shrubs are also found on Greenland; rhodora, that spreads a mist of purplish-rose across open marshy areas in late May and early June; sheep laurel, with its whorl of deep pink flowers that Thoreau called "small ten-sided rosy crimson basins"; and bog laurel, huckleberry, bilberry, and a tiny cranberry with a shooting-star-shaped flower.

Encircling the open bog is a slowly advancing succession of the boreal forest—the larch which turns soft gold in October before shedding its needles for winter, and the short-needled black spruce, both of which are found northward to the limit of trees, from Newfoundland and Labrador, across to northwest Canada and Alaska.

Other typical trees of the far north are white spruce of the island's cooler coastal shores and rocky points, paper birch that was used by the Indians for their canoes and wigwams, quaking aspen, whose flat-stemmed leaves flutter with every passing breeze, and a few isolated clumps of jack pine.

An intermediate forest is symbolized by the stately white pines with their soft blue-green needles and long pendant cones. Where trails and carriage roads lead beneath these tall trees, the air is fragrant and the wind makes a soft sound brushing through their outstretched branches. Others of this forest community are the red pine, pungent balsam fir, ancient hemlocks of lakeshores and cool ravines, northern white cedar of swampy places, yellow birch and big-tooth aspen, and of course the abundant red spruce that forms dense forests across the island where one hears red squirrels scolding and nuthatches and crossbills chattering.

It is in the shade of such a forest that one discovers a "Hobbit" world of tiny growing things: the seedlings of spruce, pine, and fir, and mats of partridge-berry and mountain cranberry, along with checker-berry, pyrola, wild lily of the valley, starflower, and masses of bunchberry whose white dogwood bracts of spring turn to bright red-clustered berries by late summer. Mushrooms of every shape and color spring up when there is sufficient rain. Mantles of haircap and other green mosses cover the ground, rocks, and rotting logs, along with gray cladonia lichens—the red-capped "British soldiers," pixie cups, staghorn, reindeer, and cloud.

Finally, the forests of Mount Desert include a variety of temperate deciduous trees, some of which range far south to the Gulf states. Among them are red and sugar maples, beech, red oak, and cherry, with a scattered few white ash and hornbeam. In the coolness of this forest are clumps of ferns—the large spreading interrupted and cinnamon, and smaller New York, beech, and oak, and occasional patches of dark evergreen Christmas. In sunny forest borders there may be patches of the pale-green hay-scented fern, while royal and sensitive grow in swampy places. It is hard to believe, looking at these delicate plants, that several hundred million years ago, long before there were maple trees or oaks or even pines, a warmer and more humid world was dominated by forests of tree ferns, such as exist today in only a few tropical regions.

One of Mount Desert's most picturesque trees is the pitch pine. It is found growing here, at the northern end of its range, along a few of the rocky coastal ledges and mountaintops. The south ridge trail up Dorr Mountain leads through open sunny groves of these gnarled bonsai-like trees growing amid patches of blueberry, huckleberry, bayberry, sweet fern, and creeping juniper that fill crevices and hollows in the lichen-covered granite.

By contrast, the pitch pines on the south ridge of Brown (Norumbega) Mountain are mixed with red and white pines, whose combined sweet aroma can almost overwhelm the hiker. As it winds upward from Lower Hadlock Pond, the trail now and then affords a pine-framed vista of Northeast Harbor and the Cranberry Islands beyond. Toward the summit the path emerges from the dense forest. From there, where the pines are dwarfed, Somes Sound lies below with the mountains of the island's west side rising beyond. Below on the east side Upper Hadlock Pond nestles in a sheltered valley beneath the rounded rocky summits of Bald Peak and Sargent Mountain.

On these and other mountaintops one discovers the

wild rock gardens of wine-leaf cinquefoil, mountain sandwort, mountain cranberry, sheep laurel, Labrador tea, mountain holly, withe rod, the rare golden heather and bearberry, and always the delicious low-bush blueberries that ripen in late July and early August.

One of our favorite hikes begins near the south end of Jordan Pond and climbs Jordan (Penobscot) Mountain. One fork follows the easy grade of the nearly treeless south ridge, while the other wends its way along the narrow ledges of Jordan Cliffs where clusters of polypody and rusty woodsia ferns and delicate blue harebells grow on the talus slides and rocky crevices.

From the 1194-foot summit of Jordan there is a vast panorama of mountains, lakes, forests, harbors, islands, and ocean. When the wind is dry and cool out of the northwest, the scene is in sharp focus, with islands visible far out to sea. Westward along the coast is Isle au Haut, twenty miles away, rising slightly higher than the other islands clustered around it. But with a southwest wind, distance recedes and haze obliterates the sharp edge between ocean and sky.

At other times we have watched in fascination as a bank of coastal fog rolls in—flowing over and around the smaller islands, pushing into harbors and bays. It may stop there or continue on up the valleys, finally enveloping the mountaintops in a dripping dampness. There are other fogs that mysteriously avoid the land and send long arms up Frenchman and Blue Hill bays until they meet at Mount Desert Narrows. And there are days when the air is filled with the intoxicating aroma of a fog bank lying unseen at sea.

The trail from Jordan dips down into the trees and across a saddle where a tranquil pond lies hidden among a ring of spruces. From there the trail begins its climb up the long slope of Sargent, the island's second highest mountain. On exceptionally clear days

Mount Katahdin, Maine's highest point at 5267 feet, can be seen more than a hundred miles to the north, rising like some great ghost above the vast expanse of mainland.

We especially enjoy the summer days of sailing around the outer islands when the ocean breeze is fresh and cool and the only sounds are the wind in the rigging and the lap of water along the sides. All around us the pointed spruces of the islands seem engraved against the sky. Cormorants crowd rocky treeless ledges, some with their angled wings outstretched to dry. Close by wave-splashed reefs, sleek gray harbor seals poke their whiskered heads above the waves to watch us pass.

A few of the smaller islands have summer cottages, and some have tiny year-round villages, where the old houses are usually clustered around a small harbor amid open meadows that sweep down to the water's edge. The people in these peaceful outer places have a special tranquillity, a love of simplicity.

Our return to home port is never twice the same. Sometimes afternoon clouds from the mainland cluster above Acadia's rocky summits. At other times we watch as sunset turns the array of peaks to glowing gold and pink. And once we returned by the light of a bright August moon, with the water still as a mirror and a low-lying mist creeping around the base of the darkly silhouetted islands.

In the warmer days of August, fields and roadsides of Mount Desert are thick with brilliant goldenrod and black-eyed Susans. Now the lily-pad surfaces of The Tarn and other shallower ponds are sprinkled with white water lilies, yellow spatterdock, and the yellow and purple bladderworts, while along the marshy edges, where pickerel frogs live, there are narrow-leaved arrowhead and the blue-spiked flowers of pickerelweed.

Once past the first of August, the woods no longer ring with the scores of bird songs that told of mating and territorial claims. Instead, there are the strident clamorings of the young, waiting to be fed or learning how to fly. Male warblers—the myrtles, magnolias, black-throated greens, and others—have lost their bright spring plumage that made them easy to identify, and this is a certain sign that autumn is now not far away. Swallows still swoop and glide over ponds and meadows in search of insects on the wing, but it will not be long before they are suddenly gone, heading south on their long flight back to Argentina and Brazil.

A Climax of Color

The feel of autumn begins with an occasional fresh, crisp day in September that hints of change. White and purple asters spread across meadows in the season's final floral color, and bracken ferns, touched by early frost, turn yellow and russet in forest clearings where mist forms at dawn. The mountain ash, a shrubby tree we spotted here and there on our summer climbs, is hung with heavy clusters of bright orange berry-like fruit. Then all of a sudden there are spots of deep burgundy and blazing crimson as red maples begin to turn in swampy places and in stream valleys.

With departure of the island's summer crowds, wildlife now seems more evident and active. Red squirrels and chipmunks scurry through the forest, their cheek pouches bulging with seeds, nuts, and berries they store away for winter. Whitetail deer, with their growing fawns, come out from secret hiding places in the deeper woods and cedar swamps to browse more freely.

The beavers, whose many dams and ponds are strung along every suitable stretch of stream, seem busier than ever. They are in a race with time as they fell aspen trees and drag the branches to their ponds for a winter food supply that will be locked with them beneath the ice. With sticks, small logs, and mud, they make last repairs on their dams and cone-shaped houses.

Once we interrupted a beaver at dusk in late September. We came upon one of the familiar drag trails across a carriage road and followed it through a screen of trees to the water's edge. Suddenly there was a loud crack as the beaver slapped his flat tail on the surface of the pond. Again and again he gave his warning to the others, while swimming impatiently back and forth. We took the hint and left him to his nocturnal tasks.

Dusk is also an ideal time to look for raccoons, skunks, and porcupines out foraging for food. Sometimes at sunset we watch a pair of prickly porkies as they shuffle here and there across a field of golden grass, peacefully nibbling on green plants. Occasionally one may spot a weasel or snowshoe hare. And there are mink that live along a few of the island's streams, while muskrats make their homes in abandoned beaver ponds. Black bears are only occasional visitors to Mount Desert—rarely seen by hikers. In the silent autumn nights the deep hooting of barred owls and the barks and yaps of red foxes drift through the forests, echoing across the valleys.

Now suddenly the forests, mountainsides, and valleys are streaked and patched with flaming colors —the varied shades of red and orange of maples, and yellow of birches and aspens. In the frosty mornings of early October, when the autumn colors are at their peak, we have gone canoeing on Echo Lake to see the sweep of color repeated in the calm surface of the water. The carriage roads are showered with falling leaves, while from the mountaintops the forest is a vast patchwork of vivid colors contrasting with the dark evergreens. The grand show may last for only a few days if strong winds or storms carry the leaves away, or it may hold for several weeks. There may be other places in the world that (almost) equal the climax of color on Mount Desert, but there is surely no place that surpasses this October exhibition.

By late in the month only lingering reminders touch the landscapes here and there—some yellow of birches on the mountainsides and the soft gold of larches in the bogs. As this last color fades away, Acadia's forests take on a subtler contrast: the dark conifers against the gray leafless trees. Cold November rains make a pattering sound on the brown leaves covering the forest floor, and thick clouds press down on the mountains. When the sun does shine, its rays cast a long-shadowed silver light across the land and sea. Daylight diminishes before the lengthening hours of wintry night.

Of Ice and Snow

A first light dusting of snow in late October or early November briefly transforms the gray bald summits of Acadia to gleaming white against the sky. We have seen Sargent Mountain from across the head of Somes Sound, Jordan from the end of little Long Pond, and Cadillac from Otter Cove after a cold front moved down from Canada, changing an overnight rainstorm to snow by dawn. All along a stretch of carriage road we found tracks of deer, snowshoe hare, fox, mouse, and others we did not know. Without the snow we would never have known these creatures had passed there.

Winters vary widely from year to year along the Maine coast. Sometimes heavy snows come in December and the ground remains covered under a thick blanket until late March. Christmas Eve of such a year brought a swirling blizzard that knocked out the island's electric power and swirled the snow into great rounded drifts. Christmas dawned clear and crisp, and the new mantle weighted down the spruce and fir trees in perfect symmetry. Out at sea scudding wisps and spires of "sea smoke" rose from the ocean's surface that was much warmer than the air. What a day it would have been for a horse and sleigh, to go exploring the back roads of Mount Desert; what a time the families of a century ago must have had on such a glittering day as this!

Another year, when no snow stayed on the ground beyond a day or so after each storm, we hiked up Pemetic Mountain on Christmas. Far below we saw the wind-patterned ice of Jordan Pond, while beyond rose the wall of ice-encrusted cliffs of Jordan Mountain. The sea glistened like liquid silver. We were not able to stay on top for long. The zero temperature and a strong north wind soon forced us down again to the shelter of the forest.

When winters are open, there is ice skating on the lakes and ponds. Gliding silently around, you can hear the eerie groaning, cracking, and booming sounds of the thick layer of ice as it expands, contracts, and settles along the shore. Fishermen set up their tiny shacks for warmth and drill through the ice in hope of bringing in a batch of fish.

Then, when the snow comes, the carriage roads —those not open to snowmobiling—become ideal for quietly exploring the winter wilderness on skis or snowshoes.

Ice storms sweep the island occasionally, and rarely the frozen rain will hold on the trees until the sun comes out. Mount Desert is then alive with a million sparkling jewels. Birches bend to the ground, pines and spruces are caked in ice, and the valleys resound with the crack and crash of falling limbs.

Just as it seems that winter may never end, that the warmth of summer will never flow back across the land, the first faint hints of spring repeat themselves with pussywillows and bird songs, and a change is in the wind.

"Everyone has a listening-point somewhere. It does not have to be in the north or close to the wilderness, but some place of quiet where the universe can be contemplated with awe."

—Sigurd F. Olson
Listening Point

The Flowing of Time

Long centuries before the white man discovered and settled the coast of Maine, the Penobscot and Passamaquoddy tribes of the Abnaki Indians made this rugged , beautiful land their own summer resort. Each spring, after planting their crops of corn, squash, and beans, most of them would leave the winter villages inland along the Penobscot and other rivers and paddle their birch-bark canoes down to the sea. At places convenient for clamming and fishing, they would set up summer encampments of wigwams built of poles and covered with bark.

Mount Desert Island, called Pemetic by the Indians, had several dozen of these camping spots, of which the one on Manchester Point at the mouth of Somes Sound was the largest. In addition to the seafood, these summering people found an abundance of wild berries, edible plants, and wildlife. At a number of these old campsites one may still find mounds of clam shells and an occasional arrow point —half-hidden reminders of the many hundreds if not thousands of years that Mount Desert has attracted summer visitors to its shores.

It is very likely that some of the many early explorers and fishermen from Spain, Portugal, France, England, and Scandinavia, who were looking for new lands and sources of wealth during the fifteenth and sixteenth centuries, may have sailed along the coast of Maine, discovering its hundreds of spruce-covered isles and sheltered bays. It is even possible that the Vikings visited this island nearly a thousand years ago.

The Florentine mariner Giovanni da Verrazano, exploring on behalf of France, sailed along the New England coast in 1524 and named the region Arcadia, after a peaceful, mountainous area of the Peloponnesus of ancient Greece. Five years later a Portuguese, Diego Ribero, labeled Somes Sound on his map as "Rio de las Montañas," making this the earliest known written reference to Mount Desert.

It remained for a French explorer, Samuel de Champlain, to provide the first positive description of Mount Desert and to identify it correctly as an island. In 1603 King Henry IV of France gave a Huguenot nobleman, Pierre du Guast, Sieur de Monts, a grant to all the lands in North America then claimed by the French crown so that he might convert the natives to Christianity. This land claim extended southward from the Canadian Maritimes to near where Philadelphia is today. The French called it La Cadie, or Acadia, derived, apparently, from Verrazano's earlier name.

De Monts sailed from France and located the first colony and trading post in his new territory on a tiny island in the St. Croix River (now the Maine–New Brunswick boundary). Champlain, who served as cartographer, recorder, and lieutenant of de Monts's expedition, set sail from this lonely outpost on September 2, 1604, accompanied by a dozen crew members and two Indian guides to explore westward along the coast.

After venturing forth into the Bay of Fundy in their small square-rigged bark or patache, they were soon enveloped by a thick fog of the kind that frequently closes around nearby Grand Manan Island. As the fog lifted, they proceeded, passing a cluster of rocky islands where they observed a colony of puffins and many other islands, reefs, bays, and harbors, which Champlain judged to be uninhabitable.

Then, on September 5, they passed close to an island "about four or five leagues long," separated from the mainland to the north by less than a hundred paces, and dominated by seven or eight mountains that had barren and rocky summits. He named it "l'Isle des Monts-deserts."

In later years Champlain explored the entire Maine coast and as far south as Cape Cod, Massachusetts, and went on to found the city of Quebec. He ultimately became known as "the Father of New France."

In 1609 another Frenchman, Marc Lescarbot, described his impressions as he sailed along the coast of Maine: "Whilst we followed on our course, there came from the land odors of incomparable sweetness, brought with a warm wind so abundantly that all the Orient parts could not produce the like." He was intoxicated, of course, by the combined fragrances of pine, spruce, and balsam fir.

The first attempt to establish a permanent community of European immigrants on Mount Desert Island occurred in 1613, just nine years after Champlain's historic visit. A group of Jesuits was dispatched from France by Madame de Guerchville who had received the Acadian land grant from Sieur de Monts. There were four priests, thirty colonists, and a crew of fifteen. Upon arriving at Mount Desert, the settlers were invited by Indian Chief Asticou, of the Manchester Point Abnakis, to set up their colony on the point opposite theirs at the mouth of Somes Sound. The group's leader, Father Pierre Biard, described this site at Fernald's Point as ideal for their needs: "This place is a beautiful hillside, sloping gently from the seashore and supplied with water from a spring on either side. There are from twenty-five to thirty acres covered with grass, which in some places reaches the height of a man." Rising behind the hillside is a small spruce-covered mountain from whose granite ledges one can see far up the sound, across to the island's higher mountains, and out to the island-dotted sea.

Just as the Jesuits were struggling to establish their new settlement, which they had named St. Sauveur, and were increasing their friendship with the Indians, disaster struck. An English ship sailed up the coast from Jamestown, Virginia, with orders to enforce England's claim to the Maine coast by driving out any Frenchmen found settling there. The Mount Desert Jesuits were attacked without warning or provocation only a few weeks after they had taken up residence on their peaceful meadow by the sea. Some of their numbers were killed during the battle. A few, including Father Biard, were taken as prisoners back to Jamestown, while the rest were forced to flag down French trading vessels for their return to France.

In spite of this setback, France continued to claim Maine, and to fight over it with England and the English colonists for nearly 150 years. Great sailing ships went back and forth along the coast, seeking out sheltered bays as staging areas for attacks on the enemy. Frenchman Bay, along the east side of

Mount Desert, was an ideal place for hidden anchorages, protected behind the Porcupine Islands.

In 1688 part of the original De Monts–Madame Guerchville grant of Acadia was given to Antoine de la Mothe Cadillac by the governor of Canada, and was later confirmed by King Louis XIV of France. It was this same Cadillac who subsequently founded the City of Detroit and became governor of Louisiana under the French. His ownership in Maine took in more than 100,000 acres—the whole of Mount Desert Island, several smaller islands, and some 30,000 acres of the mainland extending to the present town of Ellsworth.

Shortly after Cadillac's marriage to Marie Therese Guyon in Quebec, the honeymooners moved to a homesite overlooking Frenchman Bay. Among his descriptions of the island for the French court was an account written in 1692, concerning the sheltered waters leading into Southwest Harbor and Somes Sound: "The harbor of Monts-deserts . . . is very good and very beautiful. There is no sea [surf] inside, and vessels lie, as it were, in a box. . . . Good masts may be got here, and the English formerly used to come here for them."

Between 1675 and 1759 the warfare between the English and French became increasingly intense. Murders, pillages, and destruction of property were the rule. The Indians looked to the French as their friends, for they were mainly motivated by a religious zeal, while the English wanted to wipe out the native Indian tribes and their protectors so they could occupy these lands. Consequently, when the French and Indian Wars finally ended in 1759 with the defeat of French forces by British General James Wolfe on the Plains of Abraham at Quebec, it was also a turning point for the Indians, who now were forced to seek the safety of the interior wilderness of Maine.

Prominent among the colonists who were actively promoting English colonial control of Maine was the governor of the Massachusetts Bay Colony, Sir Francis Bernard. In 1761 he invited Abraham Somes, a cooper by trade, to leave Gloucester and settle on Mount Desert. Somes had already made several fishing trips "down east" to Maine and had even camped on the island. So he knew how good the offer was and promptly accepted it. In the fall of that year he sailed up the fjord later named for him and made plans to build a log cabin. The following year he brought his wife and daughters to the new homesite, thus founding the oldest village on Mount Desert Island.

In recognition of Governor Bernard's efforts to extend control to and to encourage settlement of Maine, the Massachusetts Bay General Court gave him title to the western half of Mount Desert, a gift that was later confirmed by a royal patent issued by King George III of England. In the autumn of 1762 Governor Bernard sailed to the island to examine his new grant, to draw up plans for a summer home, and to arrange to have the lands around "the Southwest Harbor" surveyed into five-acre lots for sale to prospective settlers—the first attempt at land speculation on the island.

While inspecting Mount Desert, Bernard described his trip up Somes Sound, which he called "the river": "October 7. Went up the river, a fine channel having several openings and bays of different breadths from a mile to a quarter of a mile. In some places the rocks were almost perpendicular to a great height. The general course of the river is north, 5 degrees east, and it is not less than eight miles long in a straight line. At the end of it we turned into a bay, and there saw a settlement in a lesser bay. We went on shore and into Abraham Somes' log house, found it neat and convenient, though not quite furnished, and in it a notable woman with four pretty girls, clean and orderly."

Soon other newcomers arrived from Gloucester and elsewhere in the Bay Colony to take up a new life, at Somesville, Southwest Harbor, and Bass Harbor . . . all part of a rising tide of immigration now starting to flow into Maine.

Governor Bernard's personal plans for development of Mount Desert came to an abrupt halt, however, when events leading up to the American Revolution forced him to return to England, thereby forfeiting his title to the island. Unfortunately for him, his policies as governor had been uncompromisingly in favor of British control of the colonies.

The first permanent settler of English descent on the east side of Mount Desert Island was John Hamor, who moved with his family in 1768 from Kennebunkport to Hulls Cove on Frenchman Bay. Others soon followed . . . "composed of sea-faring folk, thrifty, and self-reliant," many with names that are still familiar among island families today.

Yet the actual ownership of Maine was still an unresolved question. The English victory at Quebec had quieted only the French claim. There was still the United States–Canadian boundary to be determined. And on this rested widely differing views. British-controlled Canada strongly favored setting the international line at the Kennebec River, thus giving Canada jurisdiction over all but the western part of Maine. At the same time, there seemed some indication that the Canadians would compromise by setting the boundary along the Penobscot River, still leaving Mount Desert and eastern Maine to Canada. In no circumstances, they argued, would they consider a line farther east.

So how did Mount Desert Island end up in the United States? Its representatives rested their claim to all of Maine largely upon the earlier detailed account by Britain's own former colonial governor, Bernard. The argument proved convincing. Thus, in 1783, the boundary was finally set at the St. Croix River, and the settlers all along the coast of Maine were now assured of their allegiance to the United States.

One final note appears in history concerning the Bernards and Cadillacs: In 1785 John Bernard, the son of Sir Francis, was given the western half of Mount Desert by the General Court of Massachusetts, as an inheritance from the former governor—deserved because the son had been a stanch supporter of the American Revolution.

The following year Marie Therese de la Mothe Cadillac de Gregoire, granddaughter of Antoine Cadillac, also claimed an inheritance and was granted the eastern half of the island, largely as a gesture of Massachusetts's appreciation to France for help in the American Revolution. The de Gregoires moved from Paris and spent the remainder of their lives at Hulls Cove, counted among the 786 people living on Mount Desert Island in 1790.

By the year 1800 nearly every harbor and cove on the island had become a center for ship- and boat-building. Two- and three-masted schooners, brigs, sloops, and fishing schooners were in great demand for local fishing as well as the growing coastal trade in fish, lumber, ice, granite, and other materials.

To meet the demand for lumber, a number of sawmills were set up along the island's streams—notably on Duck Brook near Hulls Cove and at Somesville. In the area from Duck Brook to Cromwell Harbor, now the town of Bar Harbor, farmhouses were scattered here and there, and rough trails led from the surrounding forests. "Through these paths," one early newspaper account stated, the residents "dragged huge pine trees . . . to the seashore, and the music of the chisel, saw and adze transformed them into ships that sailed away to many lands."

Agriculture was another important occupation. Wheat, barley, rye, corn, potatoes, as well as vegetables and herbs, were grown by nearly every island family. And there were cattle, dairy cows, pigs, chickens, and sheep—the latter providing wool which island housewives made into clothing. In conjunction with fishing, there were many smokehouses for curing herring and other fish. There were ice-houses for storing great blocks of ice, cut from the lakes and ponds, for summer refrigeration. In short, Mount Desert people were largely self-reliant, depending, as they had to, upon local resources and their own ingenuity for their survival. Many of the islanders today still have the same qualities of down-to-earth self-reliance and independence.

In 1820 Maine ceased being part of Massachusetts and joined the Union as a separate state. Mount Desert now boasted 1349 permanent residents. The island's most important business community, then called "Betwixt the Hills," later renamed Somes-ville, had a small store, a blacksmith's shop, a shoe-maker's shop, a tanning yard, two boatyards, a bark mill, a sawmill, a lath mill, a shingle mill, a grist mill, and a schoolhouse, also used for village meetings. In 1852 the typically New England white-steepled Somesville Meeting House, which still graces the village, was erected.

In 1837 Mount Desert was finally connected to the mainland by a bridge to serve a growing number of horse-drawn carts and wagons. A toll was charged for this crossing for many years (fifteen cents for a single team and twenty-five cents for a double) until the coming of the automobile.

Meanwhile, along the seaward side of the island, navigational aids were built one by one. The first lighthouse in the vicinity was Petit Manan, just east of Schoodic Peninsula, in 1817. Its 119-foot granite tower can still be seen on a clear day from the summit of Cadillac Mountain. A lighthouse went up out on Baker Island in 1828, replaced by the existing whitewashed brick tower in 1855. Others followed: Mount Desert Rock, twenty-five miles south of Mount Desert, in 1830; Bear Island, at the mouth of Northeast Harbor, in 1839; Bass Harbor Head, on the southernmost headland of Mount Desert, in 1858; Egg Rock, guarding the entrance to Frenchman Bay, in 1875; and Great Duck Island, out beyond the Cran-

berries, in 1890. For many years these important coastal beacons, with their booming foghorns, were operated by hand, with families living at the light stations. Many are the tales of adventure, courage, and loneliness that came from the lives of these hardy people. But in recent years, under the U.S. Coast Guard, nearly all of the lighthouses have been automated, thus ending a unique chapter in the history of coastal Maine.

Summer visitation on Mount Desert began slowly in the 1840s and 1850s, when scientists, writers, and artists, including some members of the famed Hudson River School of painters, came to study and por-tray the mountains, lakes, and seashore. Thomas Cole came in 1844, followed by Albert Bierstadt, Frederick E. Church, and Thomas Birch.

Among the first written references to the island as offering an ideal summering place was an article by Robert Carter, a Washington correspondent for the New York *Tribune*. In his account of sailing from Boston to Bar Harbor in 1858, he wrote:

Before us the peaks of Mount Desert came gradually into view, at first misty and blue, then green and wooded. . . . The approach to Mount Desert by sea is magnificent. The island is a mass of mountains which seem to rise from the water. As you draw near, they resolve them-selves into thirteen peaks. . . . It is difficult to conceive of any finer combination of land and water than this view.

Carter spent the first night on the island at South-west Harbor.

Next morning . . . we hired . . . a one-horse wagon, and a quiet-looking beast, to convey us to Bar Harbor. . . . A drive of several miles over a rough mountain-road brought us to Somesville. . . . Here we dined at the house of a publican. . . . After dinner, we drove for several miles through a forest where nothing living was visible but squirrels, rabbits, partridges, and an occasional eagle. We passed no house, no sign of human handiwork, except a ruined mill. [While staying at Bar Harbor] we spent two days exploring the recesses of Otter Creek . . . and rambling the gigantic cliffs of Great Head, Schooner Head, and other bold rocky promontories rising for hundreds of feet from the sea, which make the island so fascinating to the landscape and marine painter.

He emphasized that Mount Desert was already "a favorite resort for artists and for seaside summer loungers." And so, the reputation of the island began to spread far and wide.

An account by a Mrs. Austin in 1866 sheds further light on traveling from one part of the island to another. She wrote that "the road from Southwest Harbor to Bar Harbor is set down as 16 miles in length. To this may be added some five or six miles of perpendicular ascent and precipitous descent; the latter remarkably exhilarating for strong nerves, but rather trying for weak ones, especially as the horses are encouraged to make the descents at full speed, and the pitch of the carriage and clatter of rolling stones becomes something really awful."

In those days, in contrast to today's paved highway, the ride up Cadillac Mountain offered its challenges. As Mrs. Austin described: "For pedestrians of moderate powers . . . the road up Green Mountain offers sufficient exertion to satisfy either conscience or spinal system. It can be accomplished by horse-power, if one is neither timid nor sympathetic with the brute creation." She seemed to prefer climbing on foot, "by frequent rests upon mossy logs or shaded rocks, drafts from a clear cold spring, . . . and mouthfuls of blueberries and mountain cranberries. The Summit House, reached at length, proved to be a comfortable cottage of primitive construction, but furnishing tolerable beds and a very good dinner." The building atop Cadillac was later destroyed by fire, and since then there have been no overnight accommodations.

As for other early island accommodations, the early visitors, who came to be known as "rusticators," at first took rooms at the homes of local residents or at small boarding houses and inns, such as the old Somes Tavern in Somesville, where the atmosphere was relaxed and informal and where guests sometimes joined the family of the house for meals or helped with farm chores. As the demand increased, a few simply furnished, rustic hotels were built—the Island House in Southwest Harbor, in the early 1860s, being the first because of its proximity to Mount Desert's first steamboat wharf.

Following the Civil War, tourism became more popular than before, and in 1868 a wharf was built at Bar Harbor, where Captain Charles Deering brought his steamer, *Lewiston.* Bar Harbor's first two hotels, the Agamont and Rodick House, were erected nearby, the latter expanding within the next two decades to become the largest hotel in all of New England. It accommodated more than six hundred guests.

All through the 1870s more hotels were built, while additions were made to the older ones year by year. More frequent steamboat runs were provided to meet the growing influx of summering people, with stops added at all the main harbors. The most famous of the later coastal steamboats serving Mount Desert Island were the side-wheeler *Mount Desert,* and the *J. T. Morse,* the latter operating there until the early 1930s.

In the meantime the island's most important industries, besides the blossoming summer tourist business, included fishing and lobstering, lumbering, boatbuilding, ice-cutting, and granite-quarrying. Hall Quarry, on the west shore of Somes Sound, was for many years a major rock-quarrying center. From there went the beautiful "Somes Sound Granite," destined for public and private buildings near and far, including the U.S. Mint and the Customs House in Philadelphia, and the Library of Congress in Washington. The quarry and village were named after Cyrus James Hall who founded the Standard Granite Company in 1870 and operated it for thirty years. At the peak of the quarry's activity in the 1880s and 1890s, a thousand men were employed to extract and cut some of the world's most prized granite. Limited operations finally ended in the late 1950s, and today the quarry holes and great rusting and rotting derricks and booms are all that remain of the once-bustling scene.

As tourism increased, some of the island industries began to decline—as, for instance, lumbering. With ten water-powered sawmills and two steam-powered ones in operation, nearly all of the accessible, low-lying areas of original forest on Mount Desert had been logged off. While some of these lands were growing back in second growth, nearly all areas that could be converted to agriculture were producing crops, growing hay, or supporting livestock. This landscape is in sharp contrast to that of a century later, when all but a handful of the farms have been abandoned and the fields and meadows are slowly returning to brush and woodland.

Just as the island's hotel business was continuing to grow at a rapid clip on into the 1880s—in an atmosphere of easygoing, informal manners and customs—a new trend was emerging that would soon spell doom for most of the hotels themselves. Increasing numbers of wealthy summering people from the big Eastern cities were beginning to feel the need of greater comfort and privacy than the bustling hotels were able to provide. This trend triggered a land boom in which, according to the local newspaper, the "fire of speculation . . . glowed wildly in the breast of every man and woman who possessed or could buy a piece of land." In some cases, resident landowners built cottages and rented them to summer people. But many of the "rusticators"

built their own summer cottages. At first most of these homes were rustic, simply designed places, reflecting the owner's love of the outdoor life of hiking, mountain climbing, nature study, boating and canoeing, hay rides, buckboard outings, "rocking," trail-clearing, berry-picking excursions, and other simple pleasures. Canoeing, incidentally, was then especially popular out around the islands of Frenchman Bay from Bar Harbor, and the Cranberry Islands from Seal and Northeast Harbors. Eventually a canoe club was founded and Penobscot Indians were hired to give canoeing lessons to youngsters.

Historian George E. Street, in his book on the history of Mount Desert, described those times of simple fun: "probably the island was the scene of more plain living and high thinking than any other summer resort on the coast." And another observer said that "the name of Bar Harbor was synonymous with a gay, unconventional, out-of-door existence, with merry courtships and happy irresponsible days."

One response to the growing popularity of excursions on the island was construction of a sight-seeing cog railway from the shore of Eagle Lake to the summit of Cadillac (Green) Mountain in 1883. A small steamboat brought passengers across the lake to the landing, where they boarded the tiny one-car steam-powered train. Promoters of the Green Mountain Railway were so eager for business that they dynamited holes in the old buckboard road to the summit, but the buckboard had the last say, for the rail business soon slumped off, and service ended only seven years after it had begun.

As the 1880s neared their end, more than 15,000 summer people were coming annually to Mount Desert on the Maine Central Railroad, via Bangor, Ellsworth, and a spur line from Hancock to the Mount Desert Ferry Landing on Hancock Point. Another 10,000 came on the various coastal steamboats from Rockland, Portland, Boston, and New York. Those were the days, ending in 1934, when the harbors and hills of the island echoed with shrill whistles, as the steamers brought loads of city-weary people, arriving with their great steamer trunks, pets, and all sorts of paraphernalia, for a full summer of fun. Mount Desert was then much more remote—in fact and in spirit—from the hustle of city life than it is today. In fact, the island was so far removed in time that most of the summer people then were those who could afford a two- or three-month vacation, such as college officials and professors, artists, ministers, scholars, and financiers.

During the 1880s and 1890s increasing numbers of America's wealthiest citizens began to arrive—not to live the simple outdoor life of the rusticators, but to build elaborate summer "cottages" that were actually large and elegant mansions and estates. During the Gay Nineties there were nearly two hundred of these grand cottages, set amid spacious, manicured lawns, flower gardens, and woods. Houses and grounds were served and tended by large staffs of servants: maids, butlers, footmen, and gardeners. And with these new people came a new life style—of luxury and, often, of ostentatiousness that overshadowed and smothered much of the earlier rustic atmosphere, especially in Bar Harbor. To serve these new tastes, major stores of New York and Philadelphia opened summer shops, catering to the most expensive wishes in clothing, specialty foods, and gifts.

Industrialists, politicians, ambassadors, and other socially prominent people came by the dozens with their families. Names such as Pulitzer, Morgan, Morgenthau, Vanderbilt, Astor, Carnegie, Kent, Stotesbury, Ford, and Rockefeller were familiar. And there was a merry round of elegant dinner dances, musicales, yachting parties, and gala balls. Exclusive clubs were formed for yachting, horse shows, tennis, swimming, and just plain speech-making. During the 1890s, the famous Kebo Valley Club became the island's major social center, sponsoring tournaments in golf, croquet, Ping-pong, and tennis. The biggest single summer event for many years was the annual horse show at Robin Hood (later renamed Morrell) Park. At this and many other functions the elite of Mount Desert arrived in their polished carriages and buckboards, the ladies in long, flowing dresses and broad-brimmed hats, sometimes holding parasols, and the gentlemen in suits, stiff collars, and stiff-brimmed straw hats.

Another popular social event was afternoon tea, and there were many teahouses scattered around the island for many years—among them the Tea Cup Inn, Blue Shutter Tea Room, and The Tea Garden. Of all of these, only one is still in operation: the Jordan Pond House, which the Bar Harbor *Record* reported in 1890 "is situated on a picturesque spot at the southern end of Jordan's Pond, and from it can be had magnificent views of the mountains." Beginning in 1895, under the ownership of Mr. and Mrs. Thomas A. McIntire, afternoon tea and popovers, and the renowned luncheons and dinners of charcoal-broiled chicken, topped off with "heavenly" homemade peach and strawberry ice cream, soon became a unique island tradition that miraculously continues to this day. Tea is served, as it has been for generations, at rustic tables set out on the lawn, while meals are enjoyed either on the piazza or in the birch-bark-paneled dining rooms, often before a cheerful crackling fire in the massive stone fireplaces—all in an atmosphere of the past.

The most popular horse-drawn conveyance of the 1880s and early 1890s on Mount Desert was the buckboard, and for many years these vehicles were manufactured in Bar Harbor. Some of them were small, holding three passengers, while the largest—the great tallyho—accommodated fourteen people. There are still a few islanders around who recall with nostalgia the excursions to places such as Ocean

Drive and Jordan Pond, with the spirited blowing of the long brass tallyho horn by the driver as they approached turns in the winding dirt roads. Then, as the years passed, there were other conveyances—runabouts, surries, and cut-unders, as well as the swanky carriages.

As the Mount Desert *Herald* commented: "The time was when buckboards were the only vehicles on the island. Now, almost as many handsome equipages are to be seen as at Newport." The newspaper also pointed out that "Buckboard parties are not as popular as they were. . . . The hay rides have been relinquished, and that buckboard parties are waning in favor is, perhaps, not to be wondered at, but that the boating and canoeing should decrease in popularity is more surprising."

Bar Harbor had indeed become the leading summer resort of the nation's wealthiest. Wrote a columnist for the local newspaper: "The discontented hand of progress has transformed the struggling fishing hamlet of a few years ago into a fashionable summer resort, at whose shrine the beauty, wealthy and fashion of the country pay homage."

In the words of historian Sargent F. Collier, in his book *Green Grows Bar Harbor,* "With no income tax, a plethora of servants, and eggs twenty cents a dozen, joy could be unrestrained."

1. A glacial erratic boulder. (*Butcher*)
2. Robinson Point Light, Isle au Haut. (*Menzietti*)
3. Surf along Ocean Drive. (*Menzietti*)
4. Amanita mushrooms. (*Butcher*)
5. Pemetic Mountain from the north end of Eagle Lake. (*Butcher*)
6. A Hobbit world of sphagnum moss and mushroom. (*Butcher*)
7. Jordan Pond from the Jordan Cliff Trail. (*Butcher*)
8. A spruce seedling sprouts from a crack in the granite. (*Butcher*)
9. Polypody ferns. (*Butcher*)
10. Great Pond from Beech Mountain. (*Butcher*)
11. Eagle Lake reflects a summer sunset. (*Menzietti*)
12. The makings of a blueberry pie. (*Butcher*)
13. Outer shore of Baker Island. (*Butcher*)
14. Bunchberries. (*Butcher*)
15. Rhodora. (*Menzietti*)
16. Wood lily. (*Butcher*)
17. Violets in a bed of pine needles. (*Menzietti*)
18. A Hadlock Brook waterfall. (*Butcher*)
19. A typical spruce-covered islet. (*Butcher*)
20. Seaside goldenrod. (*Menzietti*)
21. A cormorant colony on a rocky ledge at sea. (*Butcher*)
22. Mount Desert's mountains from Baker Island. (*Butcher*)
23. Water lilies. (*Menzietti*)
24. Roadside lupines. (*Menzietti*)
25. Shadbush at Great Pond. (*Butcher*)
26. Frenchman Bay from the Beehive. (*Butcher*)
27. Jordan Pond and the island-dotted ocean from the South Bubble. (*Butcher*)
28. A fern-bordered trail. (*Butcher*)
29. Irises at Asticou. (*Butcher*)
30. Pitch pines on Acadia Mountain. (*Butcher*)
31. Shadbush and the pink of new oak leaves on Acadia Mountain. (*Butcher*)
32. Great Cranberry Island from Seawall. (*Menzietti*)
33. A beaver dam. (*Butcher*)
34. Surf at Otter Cove. (*Menzietti*)
35. Pink granite along Ocean Drive. (*Butcher*)
36. Pitch pines on Dorr Mountain. (*Butcher*)
37. Autumn foliage at Upper Hadlock Pond. (*Menzietti*)
38. Jordan Pond and the Bubbles. (*Butcher*)
39. Upper Hadlock Pond and Bald Peak. (*Menzietti*)
40. A carriage path in later afternoon, looking toward Jordan Mountain. (*Butcher*)
41. Mighty breakers of a winter storm. (*Menzietti*)
42. The Tarn from Huguenot Head. (*Menzietti*)
43. Autumn turns a bracken fern to gold. (*Menzietti*)
44. The brilliant crimson of blueberry bushes in October. (*Menzietti*)
45. Blazing maples at Bubble Pond. (*Butcher*)
46. October gold of tamarack. (*Butcher*)
47. Striated rock at Norwood Cove. (*Butcher*)
48. Evening light glances along the shore. (*Menzietti*)
49. A surf "geyser" near Otter Point. (*Menzietti*)
50. Sunset strikes Marshall Brook salt marsh, with Western and Beech Mountains beyond. (*Butcher*)
51. Somes Sound and Sargent Mountain with first touch of snow. (*Butcher*)
52. A March ice storm coats every branch. (*Menzietti*)
53. Hunters Beach Head. (*Butcher*)
54. Jordan Mountains from little Long Pond, locked beneath ice and snow. (*Butcher*)
55. Ice sparkles from every twig. (*Menzietti*)

2

3

1

4

5

6

8

9

10

14

16

15

17

18

19

20

21

22

23

24

43

45

44

> "Recreational development is a job not of building roads into lovely country, but of building receptivity into the still un-lovely human mind."
>
> —Aldo Leopold
> *A Sand County Almanac*

Toward a National Park

Dawning in the minds of a few of Mount Desert's devotees at the turn of the century was a growing realization that something should be done to preserve for posterity some of the island's incredibly beautiful mountains, lakes, and seashore. In August 1901 Harvard University's president Charles W. Eliot convened a meeting in the village of Seal Harbor with railway executive George Vanderbilt, New York banker John S. Kennedy, New York businessman William J. Schieffelin, Bishop William Lawrence of Massachusetts, and a Bostonian by the name of George B. Dorr. The purpose was to organize a corporation that could acquire outstanding scenic areas on the island for the enjoyment of present and future generations in perpetuity.

Dorr was named the executive officer of the Hancock County Trustees of Public Reservations, and in 1903 the Maine legislature granted the Trustees a special tax-exempt charter that stated that the corporation was "to acquire, by devise, gift, or purchase, and to own, arrange, hold, maintain, or improve for public use lands . . . which by reason of scenic beauty, historical interest, sanitary advantage or other like reasons may become available for such purpose."

The Trustees soon received two small gifts—a rod-square plot of ground overlooking the sea near Seal Harbor for a monument commemorating Champlain's historic visit in 1604, and a summit above Jordan Pond.

No further gifts were made during the next five years, and discouragement began to set in. Then finally, in September 1908, came the first substantial acquisition—the Beehive and the Bowl, a tiny mountain and pond near Great Head, given by Mrs. Charles D. Homan of Boston.

Eliot and Dorr were encouraged by this donation. But now a new problem arose, with the invention of the portable gasoline-powered sawmill that threatened to level the island's mountain forests that had previously been inaccessible. The Trustees vowed they would next try to purchase the summit of Cadillac (Green) Mountain. With the backing of banking millionaire Kennedy, Dorr finally negotiated this exciting addition, which is today the most popular single spot on the island for visitors from all over the world.

Sieur de Monts Spring was the next purchase, snatched just seconds ahead of a group of private speculators. Then Dorr himself donated a cherished parcel of his own: Bear Brook ravine between Champlain Mountain and Huguenot Head, along with Beaver Dam Pool, which was surrounded by beautiful old hemlocks and yellow birches.

The series of additions that soon followed emerged from opposition to construction of a summer home overlooking Eagle Lake. This development, in the opinion of the Trustees, posed a threat to the purity of Bar Harbor's water supply. As a result, they were able to obtain from the state legislature the power of eminent domain, whereby they could force the sale of lands that were within the watersheds of municipal drinking water. Armed with this new authority, Dorr acquired Sargent Mountain, the island's second highest summit, and other important lands.

By 1913 the total of all holdings assembled by the corporation was just over 5000 acres. But in the midst of growing accomplishments the Trustees were suddenly faced with a crisis. A group of lobbyists, including lumbermen, were pressuring the legislature to repeal the Trustees' tax-exempt charter. While this threat was ultimately defeated, the incident so alarmed Dorr that he concluded that the "protected" lands would not really be secure for all time unless they could receive some kind of national protection. As Dorr himself later said: "It is here, the story of our National Park begins, born of an attack upon our Public Reservations charter."

Since Congress, at that time, was already faced with a number of proposals for new national parks, Dorr decided he would have better luck if he initially tried to win protection under the national monument provisions of the Antiquities Act of 1906, a law that empowers the President of the United States "to declare by public proclamation historic landmarks, historic and prehistoric structures, and other objects of historic or scientific interest . . . to be national monuments."

In 1914 the Trustees formally offered its Mount Desert acreage as a gift to the nation. It was not until two summers later, however, that Dorr finally gave up his patient waiting for the wheels of the federal government to start moving, went down to Washington, and in the company of a Maine senator and congressman met with President Woodrow Wilson, to urge him to sign the proclamation. After still more

tedious delays and uncertainties, some last-minute doubts about the legality of the gift were finally cleared up, with timely help from Harvard's Eliot. On July 8, 1916, Sieur de Monts National Monument was finally established. Logically, George Dorr was named custodian, although he initially had to serve without pay, and for some time received only a dollar a month for his services.

At the dedication of the national monument a month later, Dorr spoke of the challenges that lay ahead:

We have begun an important work; we have succeeded until the nation itself has taken cognizance of it and joined with us for its advancement; let us not stop short of its fulfillment in essential points. Adequate approaches to the National Monument, which men and women from the country over will henceforth come to see, should be secured. The areas adjoining it that are fertile in wildlife—exceptional forest tracts, wild orchid meadows, and natural wildflower areas of other types, the pools haunted by water-loving birds, and the deep, well-wooded, and well-watered valleys that lie between the mountains—are necessary to include in order to make the Park what it should be, a sanctuary and protecting home for the whole region's plant and animal life, and for the birds that ask its hospitality upon their long migrations. Make it this, and naturalists will seek it from the whole world over, and from it other men will learn similarly to cherish wildlife in other places.

That first year, which was only three years after the automobile had finally been allowed on Mount Desert Island, more than 15,000 cars and 101,000 people toured the area. In spite of this popularity, there was no money from Congress to operate the new reserve, since federal funds were being drained away to fight World War I. Dorr finally arranged a meeting with Theodore Roosevelt in April 1918, with the result that the former President wrote a letter to the Congress, appealing for funds for Sieur de Monts monument. A sum of $10,000 was promptly appropriated.

Along with this long-overdue allocation of money was a recommendation by a Congressional committee that the area be established by Congress as a national park and named in honor of the Marquis de Lafayette. This measure was quickly approved by Congress, but ran into an almost fatal delay while President Wilson was preoccupied with peace negotiations at the end of the war in Europe. Once again Dorr went to Washington in hope of expediting matters, which he did by personally carrying the bill, and a companion one establishing Grand Canyon National Park, from the Capitol to the White House. On February 26, 1919, Lafayette National Park was signed into law—becoming the first such park east of the Mississippi, the first federal area along a seashore, and to this day the only national park comprised entirely of private gifts. Dorr, naturally, was named its first superintendent.

The next major period of land expansion of the reserve relates indirectly to the admittance of the automobile on the island in 1913. John D. Rockefeller, Jr., a summer resident of Seal Harbor, had been among the stanchest opponents of the automobile. When he was defeated, millionaire Rockefeller devised a plan for laying out an entirely separate network of "horse roads," so that he and his friends could continue to ride safely in their horse-drawn carriages or on horseback. Initial construction of these graveled roads was on Rockefeller's own lands. But he soon was given special permission from Interior Secretary Franklin K. Lane to run sections of roadway through part of the newly established national park, to the south of Sargent Mountain. All went well until 1920, when a group of Northeast Harbor summer residents, led by George Wharton Pepper, voiced their opposition to the apparently un-

ending construction program that they felt was intruding upon the natural wildness of the area. Rockefeller responded to the adverse public opinion by halting his project.

Superintendent Dorr was alarmed by all the furor, for he feared it would risk losing Rockefeller's sympathetic and active help in enlarging the park. So Dorr suggested that the next stretch of carriage road should be a route "that would enable our rangers to pass readily between the northern and southern sides of our mountain range, for wildlife and woods protection if nothing more." Rockefeller agreed to this idea and also suggested extending this road in a loop around Sargent Mountain. He further proposed building a mountain road for automobiles between Seal Harbor and Bar Harbor.

Work on this package of new projects had scarcely gotten under way when new opposition arose, from a familiar source. George Wharton Pepper, now a United States senator, led the attack once again. A public hearing was held in Washington which brought such an outpouring of support and appreciation from Maine residents and friends that Pepper politely withdrew his complaint.

To avoid any further controversies over the question of building roads on federal park land, Rockefeller and Dorr made certain that proposed additions to the park were held privately during road construction. Such was the case around Eagle Lake, westward around Aunt Betty's Pond, and northward past the Breakneck Ponds and across Duck Brook. In conjunction with the fifty-seven miles of carriage roads, Rockefeller's talented crew members built sixteen architecturally delightful stone bridges, many of them real works of art. Today, as the park visitor walks, bicycles, rides horseback, or cross-country skis on these pleasant woodland roads, he may come unexpectedly on one of them, arching gracefully over a motor road or a dashing stream in some remote valley of the park. So skillfully were these constructed that they seem an integral part of the natural scene, while reminding us of a unique chapter in the history of the island.

In September 1922 Dorr first learned that one of the owners of mainland Schoodic Peninsula, across Frenchman Bay from Mount Desert, wanted eventually to give that picturesque area to the park. It took several years to clear up an estate, but finally the way was open . . . except that the donors objected emphatically to the name Lafayette. If they were going to give their holdings to the federal government, a better name must be chosen!

Dorr had always felt "Acadia" was the most appropriate name; consequently, with the Schoodic donors in agreement, the bill adding the mainland unit to the reserve also authorized the change of name to Acadia National Park. President Calvin Coolidge signed the measure into law on January 19, 1929.

Surprisingly, the famed coastline along Ocean Drive, from Sand Beach, past Thunder Hole, to Otter Point, had not yet been added to the park. But now the generous Rockefeller offered funds for this outstanding addition, at the same time agreeing to reconstruct and improve Ocean Drive, as a second segment in his ultimate plan for a Park Loop Road. But there was a string attached . . . the U.S. Naval Radio Station on Otter Point, that had been very important during World War I, must be moved off Mount Desert Island, over to Schoodic Peninsula. Not until 1935, after much haggling back and forth among federal authorities, was this move accomplished so that Rockefeller's project could proceed. Over the many years John D. Rockefeller's generosity toward Acadia National Park totaled some 11,000 acres, or roughly one-third of the park today.

Among Superintendent Dorr's final accomplishments, before his death in August 1944, was obtaining gifts of land on the island's west side, including Beech Cliff, Beech and Western mountains, and the cluster of summits along the western shore of Somes Sound.

As Cleveland Amory wrote in his book *The Last Resorts,* "Dorr was a lifelong bachelor who devoted not only his entire career, but also his personal fortune to the establishment of the Park." A small plaque at Sieur de Monts Spring says simply: "In memory of George Bucknam Dorr, 1853–1944, gentleman, scholar, lover of nature, father of this national park, steadfast in his zeal to make the beauties of this island available to all."

Only three years later disaster struck Mount Desert Island. In October, following one of the most severe summer droughts in memory, with no rain since May, flames started to spread from the old Bar Harbor town dump south of Salsbury Cove. Firemen rushed to put it out. But suddenly, on "Black Thursday," October 23, 1947, a new fire raged out of control and was whipped along by hurricane-force winds out of the northwest. As described by one witness, Sargent F. Collier: "The main thrust of the Bar Harbor fire, under a forced draft of an eighty-mile-an-hour gale, roared from Hulls Cove to Great Head beyond Sand Beach and eventually out over the sea like an orange flame thrower." The tremendous winds "flung a wide sheet of flame past all opposition. Houses in its path exploded on contact. The wall of fire leveled forests and seared mountains." Many of the island's residents, its elderly, its women and children, were evacuated, while special fire-fighting teams were flown in from various parts of the United States. The fire continued out of control for five long days, conquering new territory westward around Eagle Lake, to the Bubbles at the north end of Jordan Pond, over the north shoulder of Sargent Mountain and to the head of Somes Sound, stopping just short of Somesville. That the entire east side of Mount Desert, including the villages of Seal Harbor and Northeast Harbor, did not burn up, too, was due partly to the fire fighters' ability to bring heavy equipment into the forest on the Rockefeller carriage roads, and partly to the miraculous sudden turning of the wind.

But a great many of the more than two hundred elegant summer homes and mansions of Bar Harbor were gone—signaling the end of an era that had already begun to decline with the introduction of the federal income tax, and later with the stock market crash of 1929. Gone, too, were some 8700 acres of Acadia National Park's wild forests; but not really gone, for the miracle of nature's cycle of regrowth would slowly cover the barren and scarred land, as it had done many times before the white man had come to these shores.

In the words of Acadia's superintendent Ben Hadley in 1952: "Literally the situation looked black after the fire was past, and hope for a quick re-growth of new vegetation was dim. But Nature has done a marvelous job in reclothing the burned area, and a new forest is in the making."

Almost immediately, in fact, there were new growths of lichen and moss, of blueberry and huckle-berry and bracken fern. Then came the eager sprouts of aspen, birch, cherry, maple, and oak. Beneath the spreading canopy of broad-leaved trees were the seedlings of the slower-growing pine, spruce, and fir that will ultimately outlive the others and in a century or so become once more the dominant evergreen forest.

At the same time, whitetail deer and beavers found the new habitat more to their liking and increased their numbers. Many varieties of birds that prefer the sunnier brushy environment filled the land with their songs—among them the towhee and brown thrasher.

And so it is that, while the fire brought a night-mare of grief and destruction to Mount Desert, the island now has a greater variety of natural environ-ments, the vigorous young forest contrasting with areas of the old. From these evolving environments and the gradual changes in wildlife species and their numbers, man can learn more about the intricate relationships, balances, and sequences of the ever-changing natural world of which he is an integral part. And he can be inspired and uplifted by the won-der of it all.

Toward the Future

That so much has been accomplished in the past in the protection and careful development of Mount Desert Island is, of course, the most significant con-tribution toward the future. The blending of man's works with nature's has established a rare environ-mental quality that will set the tone for years to come.

The more than five hundred gifts of private land that have been assembled to create Acadia National Park over the years will hopefully continue to in-spire future generosity. If Congress should ever grant the National Park Service at Acadia the funds and limited authority to enter into voluntary agree-ments for the purchase of private inholdings, as is true in all other national parks, the relatively modest task of rounding out park boundaries here and there and of obtaining ecologically important pri-vate inholdings would be greatly expedited, particu-larly where landowners want to add their proper-ties to the park but cannot afford to make donations.

For many years the smaller coastal islands around Mount Desert and beyond have remained little jewels of de facto wilderness, kept that way by their isola-tion, by the private owners who have treasured them, and by the few inhabitants who have managed quietly to make a living from the sea around them. Except for the earlier years of egging and slaughter of seabirds for their feathers, described so well by Carl Buchheister in the beginning of this book, most of the hundreds of islands have remained delightful and beautiful.

In recent years, however, pressures of commercial land speculation have been rapidly moving in on Maine, accelerating all along the coast, creating unbelievable price inflation, and sending shock waves into the hearts of those who love this unique place and who want it to remain forever the unspoiled environment that it has always been.

In the words of a *New York Times* editorial, "Islands at Bay," (July 26, 1972):

Islands, symbols of escape for world-weary mainlanders throughout history, are in heavy demand and short supply these days as harried urban Americans seek the tranquillity and solitude they uniquely offer. A Maine coast real estate agent lamented a couple of years ago that he had more than two hundred customers asking for islands and only two or three to sell. An island that sold for $2000 in 1965 was on the market in 1970 at $12,000.

The pressure for island retreats is creating a development boom that could destroy the very values the escapists are seeking, for this and future generations of Americans.

In response to this threat, private individuals and organizations and public agencies have been working against great odds to save a few of these irreplaceable treasures. For instance, the National Audubon Society owns Little Duck Island near Mount Desert, and several other bird islands farther west. The Nature Conservancy has purchased or been given Turtle, Stave, and Dram islands in Frenchman Bay, and it owns fifteen other island properties along the Maine coast. The National Park Service has been given Sheep Porcupine, Bald Porcupine, and half of Bar Island just offshore from Bar Harbor and half of Baker Island in the Cranberry group. The U.S. Fish and Wildlife Service owns Seal Island near Matinicus and another bird colony near Marshall Island. The Maine Department of Inland Fisheries and Game owns Green Island off Petit Manan where there is an important eider breeding colony. Citizens Who Care has helped purchase several islands in Casco Bay near Portland for the state. And the Maine State Park and Recreation Commission owns several wild islands.

Another, more recent approach that is being applied to safeguard the coastal islands is the scenic or conservation easement. After the state legislature approved the use of this legal device in 1970, the Maine Coast Heritage Trust, with headquarters in Bar Harbor, was founded in 1971 "to provide information to island and coastal property owners concerning the alternatives which are available to them for the long-term protection of their land against inappropriate developments."

Specifically, a conservation easement, under Maine law, is a legally binding arrangement between a property owner and a governmental agency in which the owner agrees to place certain restrictions on the use and development of his land. He then gives a state or federal agency the right to enforce these restrictions, in perpetuity.

More than a score of easements on island and coastal properties in the vicinity of Mount Desert have already been donated to the National Park Service or the Maine State Park and Recreation Commission. Secured by these easements, which range from allowing modest future developments to total protection, these places have been given protection from the abuses of major land developments and exploitation that would so easily destroy their fragile beauty and ecology. At the same time, the owners continue to use and enjoy their properties, and the land remains on the local tax rolls.

The early success of the conservation easement offers much hope for the future of coastal Maine. It may even set a valuable example for other areas of the country, and it is further proof that man can live in harmony with his surroundings when he cares enough to make the effort.

Park Naturalist Programs

Visitor Center and headquarters of Acadia National Park are located at the main entrance to the park, on Route 3 just south of Hulls Cove. Staff members at the information desk provide a free map-and-descriptive folder of the park, and there is a selection of books, booklets, and trail maps for sale. During the summer months a film about Mount Desert Island is shown regularly through the day in the auditorium, and a self-guiding tape tour of the park is available for rent or sale.

Sieur de Monts Spring provides a small Nature Center Building offering a brief introduction to the park's natural history; Abbe Museum exhibiting Stone Age artifacts of the eastern woodland Indians; and Wild Gardens of Acadia displaying a variety of identified native flora. Open during the summer.

Islesford Historical Museum, on Little Cranberry Island, presents an interesting array of objects, photographs, maps, documents, and books that help portray the early life along the coast. The museum was founded in 1919 by William Otis Sawtelle, a historian and professor of physics, and it was given to the national park in 1939. It is open during the summer and early autumn.

Naturalist-guided walks and trips during the summer include: early-morning bird walks, mountain climbs, ecology and seashore excursions, and children's nature groups. Naturalists lead ocean trips aboard privately owned boats—cruises among the islands of Frenchman Bay, to Baker Island, and the Cranberry Islands with a stop at the Islesford Historical Museum. Reservations usually are required for the boat trips and for some of the more popular walks.

Illustrated evening programs are given by the park staff on a wide variety of topics at the two public campground amphitheaters—at Blackwoods and Seawall.

A self-guided nature trail at Ship Harbor on Route 102A near Bass Harbor Head, introduces the visitor to the ecology of a beautiful forest-and-seashore area.

Camping and Picnicking

Campgrounds in the park are at Blackwoods, on Route 3 near the village of Otter Creek on the island's east side; and at Seawall on Route 102A near the south end of the west side. During the summer months a daily fee is charged, stays are limited to two weeks, and during the peak season spaces are allotted on a first-come-first-served basis. Nearly a dozen privately owned campgrounds are scattered around the island outside the park—such as at the head of Somes Sound, near Salsbury Cove, north of Town Hill, at Hall Quarry, in the vicinity of Southwest Harbor, and near the bridge to the mainland. Very limited camping facilities are available on Isle au Haut, for which advance reservations are required.

Picnic grounds within the park are located at Bear Springs Picnic Area on the Park Loop Road just beyond the entrance road to Sieur de Monts Spring; Seawall Picnic Area on the shore, opposite the campground entrance on Route 102A; Pretty Marsh Picnic Area overlooking Blue Hill Bay on the island's west side, just south of Pretty Marsh on Route 102; and Thompson Island Picnic Area on Route 3 just across the Mount Desert Narrows bridge from the mainland.

Swimming

The park provides lifeguards and change facilities for swimmers at two beaches: Sand Beach on Ocean Drive, where the water is always ice-cold and the ocean's undertow may be hazardous; and the beach at the south end of Echo Lake, just off Route 102. Swimming is not permitted in Eagle Lake, Bubble Pond, Jordan Pond, the Hadlock ponds, and the southern mile of Great (Long) Pond because they are all sources of municipal water.

Boating

Canoes, rowboats, and small sailboats are ideal on the lakes and ponds in Acadia National Park. Canoe rentals/sales are provided by businesses in Somesville and Manset. Although motorboats are allowed on the larger lakes and ponds, there is fortunately a ten-horse-power limit on Jordan Pond and Eagle Lake.

Ocean sailing and cruising in the water around Mount Desert Island offer one of the most popular summertime activities. An estimated 26,000 pleasure boats of all kinds and sizes come from near and far. There are weekly summer races of the island's yacht clubs, notably of the Northeast Harbor Fleet—the largest sailing club north of Marblehead, Massachusetts. Other yacht clubs are located at Seal Harbor, Southwest Harbor, and Bar Harbor. Sailboats and motorboats may be rented by the day, week, or month from businesses in Manset, Bass Harbor, and Bar Harbor.

Deep-sea fishing excursions go out from Northeast Harbor, Seal Harbor, Bar Harbor, and Bass Harbor.

Sight-seeing boat trips, in addition to those led by park naturalists, tour Frenchman Bay from Bar Harbor, and there is twice-daily summer passenger ferry service from Southwest Harbor and Northeast Harbor out to Little and Great Cranberry Islands. The Maine State Ferry Service runs a year-round automobile ferry from Bass Harbor to Swans Island, while the Canadian National Railways runs its ferry, the *Bluenose,* from Bar Harbor to Yarmouth, Nova Scotia, for which reservations are required during the summer months. Summer visitors wishing to visit the Isle au Haut unit of the park may take the boat from Stonington on Deer Isle.

Horseback Riding

For horseback riding on the carriage roads of the island's east side, horses are for hire during the summer at Wildwood Stables, just off the Park Loop Road near Seal Harbor. On the west side, horses for exploring the gravel fire roads south of Western Mountain are provided by Seal Cove Riding Stables.

Bicycling

Some of the park's carriage roads are suitable for enjoyable bicycling, especially the loop road around Eagle Lake. Bicycles may be rented or purchased in Bar Harbor.

Gardens

Thuya Gardens and Lodge, overlooking the east side of Northeast Harbor, is a peaceful haven where the natural beauty of trees and rocky ledges blend with carefully landscaped flower gardens and lawn. Open from sunrise to sunset, June through October.

Asticou Azalea Garden, at the head of Northeast Harbor near Asticou Inn, is famed for its June-blooming azaleas of many hues. A pathway winds along the shore of a pond and through a garden that is noted for its touches of Oriental landscaping: stone detailing of footbridges and benches and a Japanese flat garden of white sand and dark pines.

Oceanarium

Have you ever watched live starfish, sea anemones, pipefish, rock and hermit crabs, sea cucumbers, lobsters, scallops, and other creatures of the sea? A series of aquaria at the Oceanarium offers such an opportunity, near the U.S. Coast Guard Station at Southwest Harbor. Open during the summer and early autumn. Modest admission fee.

Scientific Laboratories

Mount Desert Island Biological Laboratory, at Salsbury Cove, sponsors research on marine life of Frenchman Bay. Founded in 1921, in recent years it has devoted much attention to the adverse effects of pollution. A lecture series is open to the public.

The Jackson Laboratory, Bar Harbor, located just south of town on Route 3, is the world's largest research center for the study of mammalian disease and behavior. During the summer, the staff presents films and lectures which are open to the public.

Antique Cars

Dozens of automobile classics are on exhibit at the Seal Cove Auto Museum, located overlooking Seal Cove Pond on Route 102. It is open during the summer, and there is a modest admission fee.

Fish Packing

The Addison Packing Company's sardine plant at the head of Southwest Harbor, off Route 102, welcomes visitors interested in an informal tour of their packing operation.

Golf

There are three golf courses on Mount Desert: Kebo Valley Club in Bar Harbor (eighteen holes), Northeast Harbor Golf Club (nine holes), and the Causeway Club in Southwest Harbor (nine holes).

Tennis

Public tennis courts are available near the Northeast Harbor municipal pier, and there are private membership clubs in Bar Harbor, Seal Harbor, and Northeast Harbor.

Libraries

Libraries, some with a wealth of historical material, are located in Bar Harbor, Northeast Harbor, Seal Harbor, Southwest Harbor, and Somesville.

Overnight Accommodations and Restaurants

During the summer Mount Desert Island offers a wide choice of motels, inns, and other overnight accommodations. Most of these are in and around Bar Harbor, but others are scattered around the island, principally at Northeast Harbor and Southwest Harbor. Reservations are advised during the peak travel season. A few motels remain open throughout the year. Restaurants, too, are concentrated in Bar Harbor, while a few others are located around the island—at Northeast Harbor, Echo Lake, Southwest Harbor, Seawall, Bass Harbor and Seal Harbor, including the historic Jordan Pond House in the park. Information on businesses is available at the information centers at Ellsworth, on Thompson Island adjacent to the Mount Desert Narrows bridge to the mainland, at the Bar Harbor Chamber of Commerce building on the municipal pier, at the Mount Desert Chamber of Commerce building overlooking the municipal pier at Northeast Harbor, and at the Southwest Harbor Chamber of Commerce booth in Southwest Harbor.

College of the Atlantic

This small, private college, reflecting a growing national interest in ecology and the environment, was begun in Bar Harbor in 1972 with the stated objective "to study the various relationships which exist between man and his environment, including both the natural world which supports his existence and the society and institutions which he has created."

Maine Seacoast Missionary Society

This organization, with headquarters at 127 West Street, Bar Harbor, was founded in 1905 "to undertake religious and benevolent work in the neglected communities and among the isolated families along the coast and on the islands of Maine." Private contributions from people throughout the country make this unique program possible, including the operation of the Society's vessel, the *Sunbeam*, which may sometimes be seen at the Northeast Harbor municipal pier.

Geographical Statistics

Mount Desert Island

108 square miles (about 69,000 acres) in area, measuring about 15 miles at its longest (north–south), and about 12 miles at its widest.

Population: approximately 8000 permanent residents and from 15,000 to 20,000 summer residents.

Acadia National Park

54 square miles (about 35,000 acres), of which
46 square miles (about 30,000 acres) are on Mount Desert,
4½ square miles (3000 acres) are on Isle au Haut,
3 square miles (2000 acres) are on mainland Schoodic Peninsula, with smaller amounts on Baker, Bar, several Porcupines, Little Cranberry, and other islands.
46 miles of carriage roads in the park, 11 miles on adjacent private land.
150 miles of trails in the park.
Trend of Park Visitation:
1948—800,000 visits
1954—1 million
1966—2 million
1972—2.45 million
1980—3.75 million estimated projection

Mountains

Cadillac (Green)	1530 feet
Sargent	1373
Dorr (Flying Squadron)	1270
Pemetic	1248
Jordan (Penobscot)	1194
Bernard (of Western)	1071
Champlain (Newport)	1058
Gilmore	1036
Bald	974
Mansell (of Western)	949
Cedar Swamp	942
Parkman (Little Brown)	941
North Bubble	872
Brown (Norumbega)	852
Beech	839
South Bubble	766
Huguenot Head (Picket)	731
McFarland	724
The Triad	698
Acadia (Robinson)	681
Youngs	680
St. Sauveur (Dog)	679
Day	580
Gorham	525
The Beehive	520
Flying	284

Wildflower Calendar

May
- maple
- shadbush
- trailing arbutus

May–June
- rhodora
- Labrador tea
- crowberry
- purple violet

June
- bunchberry
- pink lady's slipper
- golden heather
- bluets
- wine-leaf cinquefoil
- wild lily of the valley
- blueberry
- starflower
- blue-eyed grass
- arethusa orchid
- yellow bead lily
- wild iris

June–July
- clovers
- lupine
- sheep laurel
- pitcher plant

July
- white daisy
- blackberry
- hawkweeds
- twinflower
- cranberry
- common cinquefoil
- wood lily
- round-leaf pyrola
- grass-pink orchid

July–August
- wild roses
- harebell
- yellow loosestrife
- meadowsweet
- evening primrose
- Indian pipe
- Saint-John's-wort
- steeplebush
- water lily
- sundew

August
- boneset
- spreading dogbane
- pearly everlasting
- goldenrods
- early asters

August–September
- late goldenrods
- white flat-top aster
- purple asters
- butter-and-eggs

September–October
- purple asters

Lakes and Ponds
(elevations above sea level)

Sargent Mountain Pond	1050 feet
The Bowl	415
Bubble Pond	331
Jordan Pond and Eagle Lake	274
Breakneck Ponds	253
Upper Hadlock Pond	228
Aunt Betty's Pond	210
Lower Hadlock Pond	188
Witch Hole	179
Lake Wood	136
Beaver Dam Pond	128
The Tarn	97
Echo Lake	84
Round Pond	72
Little Round Pond	70
Great (Long) Pond	59
Hodgdon Pond	43
Seal Cove Pond and Somes Pond	38
Long Pond (near Seal Harbor)	8

Native Trees

eastern white pine	eastern hophornbeam
red or Norway pine	American beech
pitch pine	northern red oak
jack pine	bear oak
larch or tamarack	hawthorn
red spruce	witch hazel
black spruce	black cherry
white spruce	pin cherry
eastern hemlock	common chokecherry
balsam fir	American mountain ash
northern white cedar	shadbush or serviceberry
black willow	sugar maple
quaking aspen	red maple
bigtooth aspen	mountain maple
balsam poplar	striped maple or moosewood
yellow birch	
paper birch	alternate-leaf dogwood
gray birch	white ash
speckled alder	black ash

Native Birds
(Seasonal groupings ignore uncommon or unusual exceptions)

Permanent Residents	ruffed grouse	downy woopecker
common loon	great black-backed gull	blue jay
black duck	herring gull	raven
common eider	black guillemot	crow
white-winged scoter	great horned owl	black-capped chickadee
common merganser	barred owl	red-breasted nuthatch
red-breasted merganser	hairy woodpecker	brown creeper

robin
golden-crowned kinglet
pine siskin
American goldfinch
red crossbill
white-winged crossbill
slate-colored junco
white-throated sparrow
song sparrow

Summer Residents
double-crested cormorant
great blue heron
green heron
American bittern
least bittern
wood duck
ring-necked duck
red-tailed hawk
broad-winged hawk
bald eagle
osprey
sparrow hawk
killdeer
woodcock
spotted sandpiper
common tern
Arctic tern
mourning dove
black-billed cuckoo
common nighthawk
chimney swift
ruby-throated hummingbird
belted kingfisher
yellow-shafted flicker
yellow-bellied sapsucker
eastern kingbird
great crested flycatcher
eastern phoebe
yellow-bellied flycatcher
Traill's flycatcher
least flycatcher
eastern wood pewee
olive-sided flycatcher
tree swallow

bank swallow
rough-winged swallow
barn swallow
cliff swallow
house wren
catbird
brown thrasher
wood thrush
hermit thrush
Swainson's thrush
veery
ruby-crowned kinglet
cedar waxwing
solitary vireo
red-eyed vireo
black-and-white warbler
Tennessee warbler
Nashville warbler
parula warbler
yellow warbler
magnolia warbler
black-throated blue
myrtle warbler
black-throated green
blackburnian warbler
chestnut-sided warbler
bay-breasted warbler
blackpoll warbler
palm warbler
ovenbird
yellowthroat
Wilson's warbler
Canada warbler
American redstart
bobolink
red-winged blackbird
common grackle
cowbird
scarlet tanager
rose-breasted grosbeak
indigo bunting
purple finch
rufous-sided towhee
savannah sparrow
sharp-tailed sparrow

chipping sparrow
field sparrow
swamp sparrow

Winter Residents
red-throated loon
red-necked grebe
horned grebe
great cormorant
greater scaup
common goldeneye
bufflehead
old-squaw
surf scoter
common scoter
purple sandpiper
evening grosbeak
pine grosbeak
common redpoll
tree sparrow

Transients, Spring and/or Fall
Canada goose
mallard
green-winged teal
blue-winged teal
lesser scaup
semipalmated plover
black-bellied plover
ruddy turnstone
common snipe
greater yellowlegs
lesser yellowlegs
pectoral sandpiper
least sandpiper
short-billed dowitcher
semipalmated sandpiper
sanderling
northern phalarope
Bonaparte's gull
Philadelphia vireo
mourning warbler
rusty blackbird
fox sparrow

Uncommon or Rare
(a few others, not
listed, have been
recorded only once)
arctic loon
eared grebe
pied-billed grebe
sooty shearwater
greater shearwater
Manx shearwater
Leach's petrel
Wilson's petrel
gannet
common egret
snowy egret
cattle egret
little blue heron
black-crowned night heron
brant
snow goose
Barrow's goldeneye
harlequin duck
king eider
ruddy duck
hooded merganser
Cooper's hawk
goshawk
sharp-shinned hawk
rough-legged hawk
red-shouldered hawk
golden eagle
marsh hawk
gyrfalcon
peregrine falcon
pigeon hawk
Virginia rail
sora rail

coot
piping plover
golden plover
whimbrel
solitary sandpiper
pomarine jaeger
parasitic jaeger
glaucous gull
Iceland gull
ring-billed gull
laughing gull
black-legged kittiwake
roseate tern
Caspian tern
black skimmer
razorbill auk
common murre
thick-billed murre
dovekie
Atlantic puffin
yellow-billed cuckoo
snowy owl
hawk owl
short-eared owl
saw-whet owl
whippoorwill
pileated woodpecker
red-bellied woodpecker
red-headed woodpecker
black-backed three-toed woodpecker
northern three-toed woodpecker
western kingbird
horned lark
purple martin
gray jay
boreal chickadee
white-breasted nuthatch

Carolina wren
long-billed marsh wren
short-billed marsh wren
mockingbird
varied thrush
gray-cheeked thrush
eastern bluebird
blue-gray gnatcatcher
bohemian waxwing
northern shrike
loggerhead shrike
yellow-throated vireo
warbling vireo
worm-eating warbler
golden-winged warbler
orange-crowned warbler
Cape May warbler
pine warbler
prairie warbler
northern water thrush
Connecticut warbler
yellow-breasted chat
eastern meadowlark
yellow-headed blackbird
orchard oriole
Baltimore oriole
summer tanager
cardinal
blue grosbeak
dickcissel
vesper sparrow
lark sparrow
Oregon junco
white-crowned sparrow
Lincoln's sparrow
Lapland longspur
snow bunting

Native Mammals, Reptiles, and Amphibians

Mammals

black bear (rarely seen)
raccoon
long-tailed weasel
mink
river otter (rare)
striped skunk
red fox
bobcat (rare)
harbor seal
woodchuck (rare)
eastern chipmunk
eastern gray squirrel (uncommon)
red squirrel
northern flying squirrel
beaver
muskrat
porcupine
snowshoe hare
whitetail deer
harbor porpoise
several kinds of shrews, moles,
    bats, voles, and mice

Reptiles

snapping turtle
musk turtle
painted turtle
red-bellied snake
garter snake
ringneck snake
smooth green snake
milk snake

Amphibians

American toad (uncommon)
spring peeper
gray tree frog (uncommon)
bullfrog
green frog
pickerel frog
leopard frog (?)
wood frog
salamanders (several kinds)

Further Reading

A.M.C. Trail Guide to Mount Desert Island and Acadia National Park. Boston: Appalachian Mountain Club, 1971.

Bond, James. *Native Birds of Mount Desert Island and Acadia National Park.* Philadelphia: The Academy of Natural Sciences of Philadelphia, 1971.

Butcher, Devereux. *Exploring Our National Parks and Monuments.* Boston: Houghton Mifflin Co., 1947, 1969.

————. *Our National Parks in Color.* New York: Clarkson N. Potter, 1965, 1968, 1973.

Carson, Rachel. *The Edge of the Sea.* Boston: Houghton Mifflin Co., 1955.

Chapman, Carleton A. *The Geology of Acadia National Park.* New York: The Chatham Press, Inc.– The Viking Press, Inc., 1962, 1970.

Collier, Sargent F. *Acadia National Park: George B. Dorr's Triumph.* 1965.

————. *Green Grows Bar Harbor: Reflections from Kebo Valley.* 1963.

Coman, Dale Rex. *The Native Mammals, Reptiles and Amphibians of Mount Desert Island, Maine.* 1972.

Dorr, George B. *Acadia National Park: Its Origin and Background.* Bangor, Maine: Burr Printing Co., 1942.

————. *Acadia National Park: Its Growth and Development.* Bangor, Maine: Burr Printing Co., 1948.

Eliot, Charles W. *John Gilley of Baker's Island. The Century* Magazine, 1899. Philadelphia: Eastern National Park and Monument Association, 1967.

Favour, Paul G., Jr. *Checklist of the Birds of Acadia National Park.* Bar Harbor, Maine: Acadia National Park, 1969.

Hale, Richard W., Jr. *The Story of Bar Harbor.* New York: Ives Washburn, Inc., 1949.

Jewett, Sarah Orne. *The Country of the Pointed Firs.* Boston: Houghton Mifflin Co., 1925. New York: Doubleday Anchor Books, 1956.

Mitchell, Edwin Valentine. *Anchor to Windward.* New York: Coward–McCann, Inc., 1940.

Morison, Samuel Eliot. *Samuel de Champlain: Father of New France.* Boston: Little, Brown & Co., 1972.

————. *The Story of Mount Desert Island.* Boston: Little, Brown & Co., 1960.

Rich, Louise Dickinson. *The Coast of Maine: An Informal History.* New York: Thomas Y. Crowell Co., 1956.

————. *The Peninsula.* Philadelphia: J. B. Lippincott Co., 1958. Riverside, Connecticut: The Chatham Press, Inc., 1971.

Sharpe, Grant W. *A Guide to Acadia National Park.* Illustrated by Jane Ingraham Rupp. New York: Golden Press, 1968.

Sharpe, Grant and Wenonah. *101 Wildflowers of Acadia National Park.* Seattle: University of Washington Press, 1963, 1970.

Street, George E. *Mount Desert: A History.* Boston: Houghton Mifflin Co., 1905.

Tilden, Freeman. *The National Parks.* New York: Alfred A. Knopf, Inc., 1951, 1968.

Private Organizations Helping to Save the Maine Coast

Citizens Who Care, Box 388, Pearl Street Station, Portland, Maine 04112.

Coastal Resources Action Committee (environmental lobbying), 465 Congress Street, Portland, Maine 04111.

Conservation Law Foundation, Statler Building, Park Square, Boston, Massachusetts.

Friends of Nature, Brooksville, Maine 04617.

Maine Audubon Society, 57 Baxter Boulevard, Portland, Maine 04101.

Maine Coast Heritage Trust, Box 4, Bar Harbor, Maine 04609.

National Audubon Society, 950 Third Avenue, New York, New York 10022.

Natural Resources Council of Maine, 20 Willow Street, Augusta, Maine 04330.

Nature Conservancy, The, 1800 North Kent Street, Arlington, Virginia 22209.
  Maine Chapter, Manchester, Maine 04351.

Sierra Club, 1050 Mills Tower, San Francisco, California 94104.
  Maine Regional Group, Box 1324, Bangor, Maine 04401.

''The basic thing that so many of the prophets keep forgetting is rhythm, the cycles. That, and the fact that change is the one constant. If they hadn't alienated themselves from the land they would know these things almost by instinct.''

—Hal Borland
Homeland: A Report from the Country